virtual architecture

Conway Lloyd Morgan

Giuliano Zampi

virtual architecture

McGraw-Hill

New York   Washington D.C.   San Francisco
Montreal   Toronto

First published 1995

Designed by Marcpress
Typeset by Wandsworth Typesetting in Avenir
Printed in Hong Kong

for the publishers
B.T. Batsford Ltd.,
4, Fitzhardinge Street,
London W1H 0AH

Library of Congress Cataloging-in-Publication Data
Zampi, Giuliano.
    Virtual architecture / Giuliano Zampi, Conway Lloyd Morgan,
        p.   cm.
    Includes index.
    ISBN 0-07-072722-8 (hardcover)
    1. Architectural design–Data processing. 2. Computer-aided
    design.   I. Morgan, Conway Lloyd.   II. Title.
NA2728.Z36   1995
720'.28'4028553–dc20   95-37204
                                                        CIP

This edition published in North America by
McGraw-Hill, a division of McGraw-Hill
Companies, Inc.

ISBN 0-07-072722-8

Title page design:
the Visitor's Centre
at Cardiff Bay,
designed by Will
Alsop of Alsop &
Störmer and
visualised by
Giuliano Zampi.

Contents

Authors' acknowledgements

This book has been put together in an appropriately virtual fashion, between one author based in London and the other in Hong Kong. Most of the text was drafted in London, and faxed and refaxed back and forth. The authors owe a debt of gratitude to Janet Turner of Concord, who first introduced them, and to Richard Reynolds at Batsford, who accepted stoically this unusual way of working.

The authors would also like to thank the following for their time and interest in the project, and for supplying illustrations and permitting them to be used.

Will Alsop, Alsop & Stormer;
Stuart Rand Bell;
Dennis Caldwell, CODEC;
Enrico Checchi, ATMA, Milan;
David Clarke and Tim Brown, Autodesk;
Craig Downie, Studio Downie;
Pierre du Pont, Division;
Hans Werner Eirich, IEZ;
Terry Farrell, Terry Farrell & Partners;
Richard Frisch, Han Dataport;

Michael Hopkins & Partners;
Infobyte/ENEL, Rome;
Jonathan Ingram, Reflex Systems;
Gábor Kazár Graphisoft;
Jean Nouvel, Architectures Jean Nouvel;
Tom Porter;
Star Informatic;
George Stevenson and Tim Aikin, Engineering Technology;
Maggie Templeman and Roger Frampton, Superscape;
Keith Williams and Terry Pawson, Pawson Williams;
Peter Zwick and Axel Stockmar, Light Consult.

Special thanks also go to Martin Pawley and his colleagues at *World Architecture*, in whose columns a number of the ideas suggested here were first aired.

Conway Lloyd Morgan, London
Giuliano Zampi, Hong Kong
May, 1995

building

Building the enchanted castle

Building the enchanted castle

The dream of walking into a painting is a common fancy - finding out what the *Mona Lisa* would look like in profile, for example, or moving around the interior landscape of a painting by Ernst or Magritte. Imagine getting within the walls of the enchanted castle in Claude's famous canvas, with its facade of huge windows but no doors, and the hint of further courtyards and towers behind it. Logically we know this kind of voyage to be something impossible, psychologically we wish we could undertake it.

At the VR 94 exhibition in London, however, such a voyage was on offer. A group of Italian computer experts and designers had created, for the ENEL (the Italian electricity board), a computer visualization of the Giotto chapel in the Basilica of St Francis in Assisi. The ENEL had just installed a new lighting system in the chapel, and commissioned the Italian company Infobyte to make a virtual image of the chapel to celebrate this. Using special eyeglasses, the spectator sees the interior of the church in three dimensions on the computer screen, and can move the viewpoint using a multi-directional mouse. The quality of the imaging is excellent, and the sense of motion good, effects achieved by using not one but two CPUs in tandem.

The frescoes by Giotto in the chapel, painted at the beginning of the 14th century, depict scenes from the life of St Francis of Assisi. They are executed in vivid detail and against a background of landscapes and townscapes painted in fantastic colours: the buildings are in gold, turquoise, rose, cream and burgundy. The architecture created by Giotto is a fanciful mix of classical elements and mediaeval features: an

Claude: The Enchanted Castle (National Gallery, London)

open temple with classical pediment and Corinthian columns looks over a crenellated wall, pierced with round Norman arches, for example. On the computer screen, the frescoes were accurately reproduced, with good colour values: as each area of the chapel is reached the lighting effects switch on. But this is only the first stage. The viewer is able not only to approach the frescoes, but enter them: push forward on the mouse and you are propelled into a fantastic townscape, into the architecture that never was of a city that is not. It has been based on the visual evidence in the paintings, and disposed into a series of streets and squares which recall the perspectives of the frescoes. And the rich and unusual colours in the frescoes are found here also.

Buildings of which only a corner is glimpsed in the fresco are here found in the round, including a curious circular building topped with a gold and red barber's pole tower, based on the decorative elements in the *Trial by fire*

The Giotto Chapel at Assisi,
recreated in VR by Infobyte, Italy

fresco. Many of the building details are taken from the view of Arezzo, in the fresco of *St Francis driving out the devils* from that town. While the elements of the buildings are taken from the paintings, the arrangement and placing of them is wholly imagined. In one piazza a fountain tinkles in the sunlight, and over and around the whole townscape flies the image of a winged horse, our guide into this imaginary realm. This idea of creating a virtual city, using a painted one as a starting point, has a compelling interest, charm, even, and for all that it uses contemporary technology it is an answer to an age old dream.

The notion of creating a vision of a building before it is built is a long-standing one in architectural practice, the creation of perspective views and suchlike running parallel to the making of working drawings. Perspective drawing, particularly in the 19th century, reached heights of considerable accomplishment - many architects were themselves skilful painters. Perspective drawings were often used to show the client how the future building would look: they are still so used in some practices today. But this need to visualize a building in advance is not merely a device for presenting a project to a client, but a necessary and real part of the creative process of architecture. Imagined architecture is an important mental construct, a means of testing and evaluating architectural processes, even in 'unbuildable' situations. Imaginary architecture is not only pure design, it is also pure architecture. Not surprisingly, the advent of new technologies, including television and the computer, gave an added stimulus to this process, suggesting that not only could single-viewpoint images be constructed on the screen, but that the user could change

Two views within the Giotto frescoes, an
imaginary landscape created by Infobyte

viewpoint and even position relative to the building, and move from exterior to interior, with increasing degrees of realism.

While it took time for computers to achieve the level of presentation of images found in traditional drawings, there was one other use to which they could be put more rapidly. This was the creation of working drawings, plans, elevations and sections. We will look at the history of CAD more fully in the following chapters, but it is worth noting now that this dichotomy between different applications was to take some computer applications down a misleading path. The use of the computer to produce simple drawings made the machine into a useful workhorse, particularly on large-scale projects, which would otherwise require a great deal of drafting time. But this substituted use for function, with consequences that we will see more fully later.

The use of computers as drawing machines is now familiar to many architects, and there is little debate about their efficiency and value in this field. The use of computers as thinking machines, however, is a different matter. The potential of computers has, according to some, hardly been appreciated in the architectural community at large. This is partly a result of the way in which CAD (computer-aided design) programs have been constructed, partly the result of the late introduction of CAD into the architectural teaching and training syllabus. One of the aims of this book is to even up the debate, and show architects and those in the building profession how computers can be best put to work.

VR gets to work: the virtual lecturer, from Division (*above*) and two military applications, also by Division (*facing*)

With the introduction of Virtual Reality systems in the late 1980s a further window of opportunity opened for architects: indeed several of the early research and development applications of VR were specifically architectural, notably the Sitterson Hall environment at the University of North Carolina. Immersive VR, where the user dons a helmet and dataglove to explore quasi-physically the virtual environment, has evident architectural applications, allowing architect and client to see and use a building before construction work even starts. There are limitations to such visualizations, of course, largely related to the processing speeds and memory size of the systems used, but the basic principles are now established, and these developments are in hand.

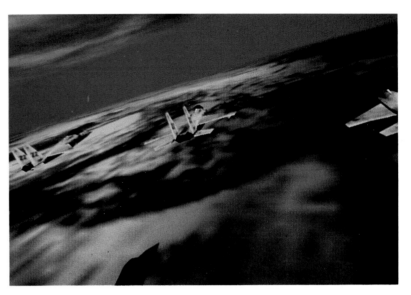

On-screen VR, where the environment is explored by means of a screen interface, is also a useful architectural tool - Real Time Design's creation of the future Quayside development in Newcastle-upon-Tyne is one of the most ambitious examples to date - allowing the chance to study and modify building plans before execution. The recent development of three-dimensional visual systems using special eyeglasses enhances the effect of perceiving architectural spaces. But as with immersive VR, the amount of memory required to maintain the on-screen image has until now limited the wider, alternative uses to which the system can be put. In this respect, VR represents a closed system, as does ordinary CAD, in its practical applications. At the same time, the concept of virtual environments in which the laws of physical space can be disregarded - the idea of cyberspace - is also tremendously important

as a generator of ideas for architects and, indeed, all others concerned with the built environment. Cyberspace - a concept first defined in the elegant and eloquent novels of William Gibson, *Neuromancer*, *Count Zero*, and *Mona Lisa Overdrive* - predicates a virtual world where humans interact directly with data, and in which the interface between physicality and software implodes. It offers a vision of an environment in which personalities become constructs, and time and space cease to have conventional meaning. The fact that the actual creation of cyberspace may be some considerable time in the future does not detract from the value of cyberspace as an intellectual model applicable to the contemporary world, in which information and information systems grow in importance and complexity, ousting traditional artefacts and communications media in an electronic revolution whose effects are all around us. The new ways of living, working and thinking forced upon society by the new media have important consequences in many areas, not least in architecture. The practical limitations and relevance of presently available systems for architectural use must not preclude consideration of the conceptual importance of cyberspace as a means of learning and understanding the challenges of the modern electronic world.

All these systems - CAD, immersive VR and screen-based VR - address the practical needs of one particular, though important, architectural task, that of visualization. The traditional methods - drawing plans, elevations and sections - that these systems supplant in fact meet a number of other, equally important needs - establishing a construction method, allowing

Two CAD projects by Giuliano Zampi, created using Sonata on a Sun workstation: an office interior for Telecom Asia (*above*) and a visualization of Will Alsop's Cardiff Bay Visitor's Centre (*facing*)

the calculation of loads and stresses, and permitting cost estimates to be generated, among others. It is actually more difficult to solve these problems using CAD and VR than it is with traditional methods. Thus parallel computer systems have been developed for these tasks, which are used by structural engineers and construction firms to handle their different aspects of the whole building task. These have started by looking at the problem in terms of the organization of information, through accessible database structures.

This book explores some of the many currently available CAD systems for architecture. The starting point has to be AutoCAD, probably the most widely-used PC application, both among architects and other design professionals. Then there are the newer, powerful rendering tools, such as Electric Image and 3D Studio. These allow surface effects and textures to be added to three-dimensional drawings for greater realism. This leads to VR systems such as Division and Superscape, and understanding what their potential is for architects, particularly in the planning of complex interior designs. Finally, what can be called final-generation CAD systems, that allow all aspects of the building process to be handled on one system, must be considered. In such systems visualizations and databases converge into a powerful working tool. Here an important model is Sonata, and the new program, Reflex. As we shall see, such programs require a different functional base to customary graphic-based systems, and offer a wide range of additional facilities, as well as detailed visualization, to the user. The importance of such systems, and their potential for handling the increasingly complex buildings now being designed and built, is evident, particularly if the architect is to remain the team leader in the creation of new buildings.

The main sections of the book show how architects have and can put all these systems, including the existing final-generation ones, to practical use, through a series of worked examples of actual applications. The final chapter looks at the wider potential for the new systems, and their influence on the future development of architecture and building.

A brief history of CAD

John Walker, the creative genius behind Autodesk, set out a few years ago a view of the development of computing which moves beyond the habitual distinctions between hardware and software, and away from the obsession with chip speed and memory size, and which instead centres on the notion of the computer as a human-machine interface. In other words, rather than considering the functional aspects of the computer, Walker's analysis concentrates on the use of computers, and their relationship with the operator. Instead of the idea of user and machine as somehow independent entities, Walker realizes that the computer is a tool which has no sense without its operator, and so the development of computing should be considered in terms of this interface, and its increasing depth of interpenetration between machine and human.

Walker suggests a taxonomy for five generations of computing. Firstly the plugboard - the computer as switchboard: capable of performing only a limited set of instructions. Then punched card machines - greater data handling, and more complex routines. Thirdly the keyboard and screen: a major move towards integration in which commands could be directly input and modified. Fourthly, the menu driven program, in which the user is even closer to the machine, not needing to memorize complex commands and routines. The fifth level is the graphic user interface, the current state of technology, in which a mouse is used to point and click. And according to Walker, the next and so the final level will be virtual reality, in which user

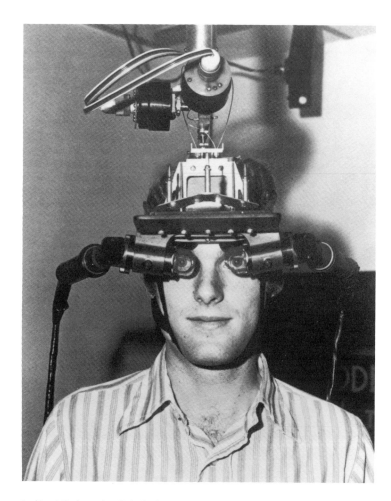

Looking at the future: Ivan Sutherland, pioneer developer of Virtual Reality, demonstrating an early helmet fitted with television screens before the eyes

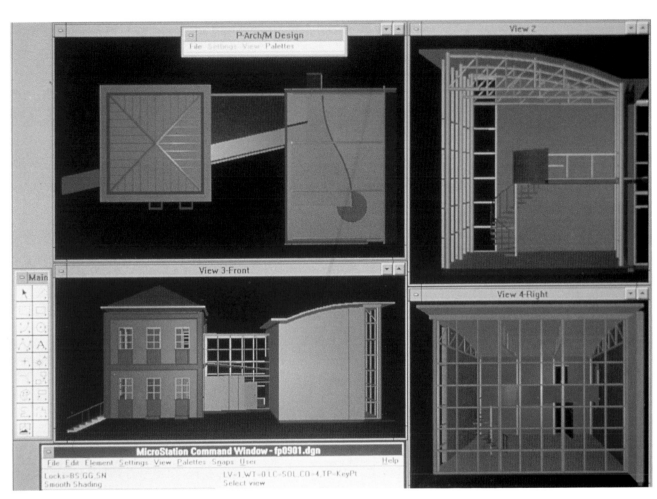

Looking at the present: a typical
working CAD screen, in this case by
Intergraph

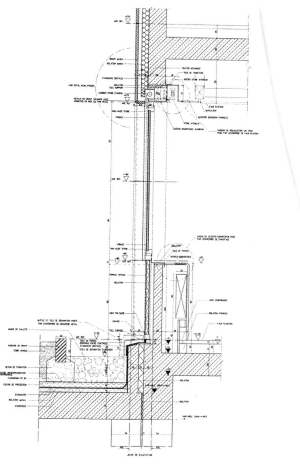

COUPE B
ECH:1/10

2D drawings: structural details by Ballini & Pitt Architectes in Luxembourg and (facing) sections through a new building in Brussels by the Loebermann office in Nuremberg

and machine coalesce into a single cyber-space entity.

We will discuss virtual reality later in this book: what Walker was drawing attention to was the way in which computers have developed closer and closer links with the user. Faster chips and larger memory are only the means to this end. This approach also discounts totally the notion of the computer as an independent 'intelligence', but also makes it more than a passive tool. It also shows that the notion of an exchange of information with a computer - the user-friendly conversation with the machine - misses the point of what is really going on. In Walker's words 'when you're interacting with a computer, you are not conversing with another person. You are exploring another world.' The world opened up by the computer is not just an extension of the real world, it can be an independent world in itself, and to see it through the perspective of the real world only is to exclude this potential added dimension. As Walker also says about computer aided design: 'CAD isn't just about drawing things with computers. It's about designing every manufactured object we use.' The CAD revolution is having effects on the material world of far-reaching importance: to see the computer as only an extension of the drawing board is to ignore vital aspects of this.

The first CAD programmes for architecture perhaps cloaked this potential with their complexity and slow speed of operation. As early as 1962, for example, SLS Environetics in Chicago began development of the Man-Mac machine, intended to draft plans for interior office spaces. Here the purpose was to remove the routine aspects of drawing plans from the

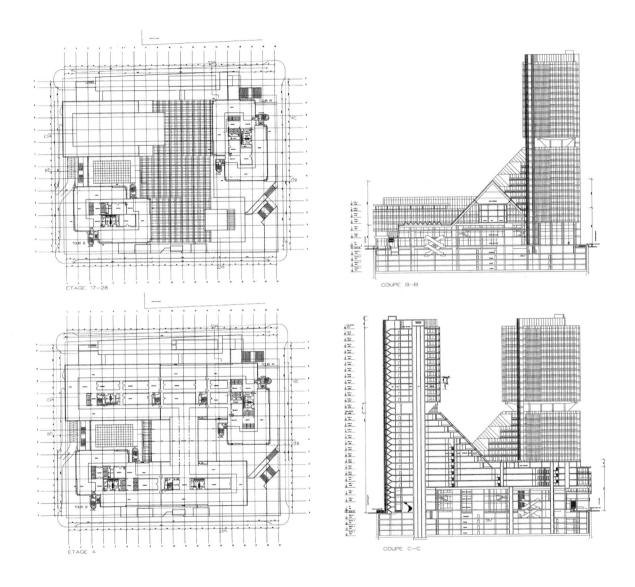

ETAGE 17-28

COUPE B-B

ETAGE 4

COUPE C-C

23

architects, freeing their time for creative work. The investment in building this specific machine was worthwhile given the volume of interior planning work to be done, but extending it into more general applications, and certainly into design, would not have been realistic with the then available levels of technology.

The development of these general applications had to wait for the arrival of the personal computer, that is to say a stand-alone system comprising input and display systems (a keyboard, screen and disk drives), a central processing unit, and integral memory (either hard or floppy disk). These machines have transformed the workplace, and increasingly they are transforming the home as well. They are now so familiar that it is difficult to remember that they have only leapt into view in the last twenty years. And in those two decades the computing power, available memory and quality of output have increased multifold. Fifteen years ago a typical personal computer would have had 32K of RAM, and two floppy drives with 360K of memory on each disc. This book has been written on a machine with 8 megabytes of RAM and 130 megabytes on the hard disc, and already it feels antediluvian!

The first computer-aided design programs used simple algorithms to display patterns of lines at first in two dimensions, and then in three. This seems like a fairly simple evolution, but a moment's thought shows that moving from a single plane to a three-dimensional space involves considerable extra memory and much more sophisticated programming. And being able to manipulate the pattern of points to see the image from different view-

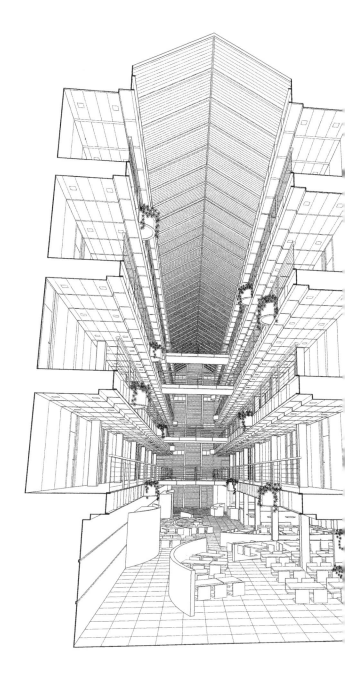

Perspective wireframe drawings for a commercial
interior by Guex + Favero in Geneva. This composite
drawing was created in Star Archi and won second prize
in the 1994 Star awards

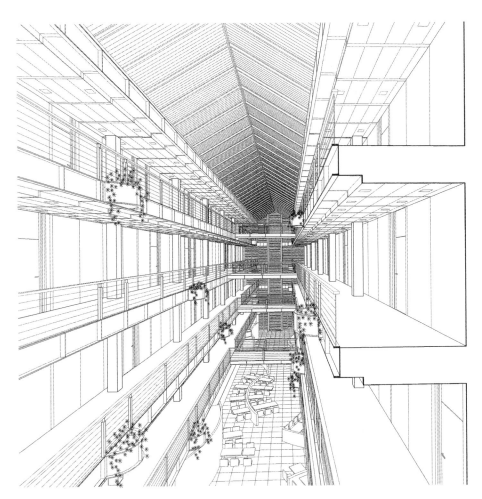

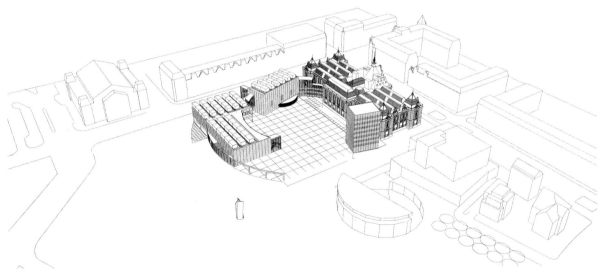

Designs for the extension of the Stedelijk Museum in Amsterdam by Architektenburo QUIST in Rotterdam, executed in Star Archi (*above & facing*)

points, and in perspective, is also a task requiring a quantum leap in the computer's capacity. Seen from this viewpoint, early work, for example by Professor Charles Eastman at Carnegie-Mellon University, is remarkably advanced, even if the monochrome wireframe images his team produced now seem tame. The Building Description System is a library of several hundred thousand architectural elements, which can be assembled and drawn on screen into a complete design concept. This can be viewed and output in different scales and levels of detail, and from perspective and planar viewpoints.

The design questions Eastman set out to answer still reflect continuing needs in computer-aided design. The idea of evaluating a concept from an available library of elements, which could be changed and modified on screen, is a key point. Another is the possibility of viewing the resulting image not only in the formal plan, elevation and section familiar to architects but also in perspective. The latter in effect encouraged the architect, Eastman believed, to look at design in different and new ways. His work laid a cornerstone - even if only one of white lines - for the coming changes in architectural design to be wrought by the computer. And it should be said that Carnegie-Mellon University is still in the forefront of computer hardware and software development, currently working with the Media Lab at MIT on developing multi-user environments for virtual reality systems, among other applications.

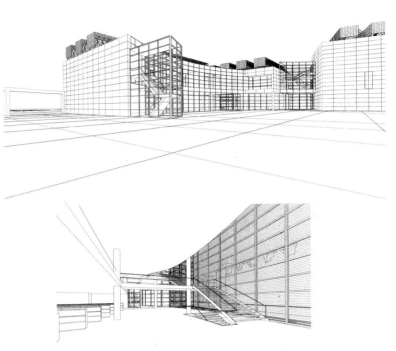

CAD : a user's guide

CAD - a user's guide

Nicholas Negroponte has written recently of the distinction between atoms and bits, both in his recent book *Being Digital* and in his column in *Wired* magazine. His point is that the traditional tendency to measure the world by its physical characteristics is increasingly irrelevant. Rather than counting material atoms, he argues, we should be looking at bits - the information content. One example he gives of this distinction is how, when visiting an integrated circuit company in America, an officious receptionist asked him for the model, make and value of the laptop computer he was bringing into the building. 'Roughly one to two million dollars' was his reply. 'Oh, that cannot be, sir,' she replied, looking down at Negroponte's old PowerBook, and writing the sum of $2,000 on her form. She was confusing atoms: the material of the computer, with bits, the software and information files inside it. Most people outside the computer world (and some inside it) make the same kind of category mistake. It is a serious issue, one which affects important problems about matters such as copyright and ownership of information, and which poses wider questions about how we are to create value judgements in an information-based society.

Computer program manuals may not have helped this distinction! They have grown in size and extent as the programs themselves have become more powerful and more complex. At the same time, there has been something of an inversion. Time was when a flimsy manual accompanied a pile of discs. Now a fat manual, sometimes in several volumes, is accompanied by a single CD. It is almost as if the software makers are deliberately increasing the size of the manuals - the atoms - to justify the importance of the bits - the product, particularly as most programs have well-organized help files included.

The development and broad application of Windows software, along with the point, click and drag graphical user interface has also tended to obscure bits behind

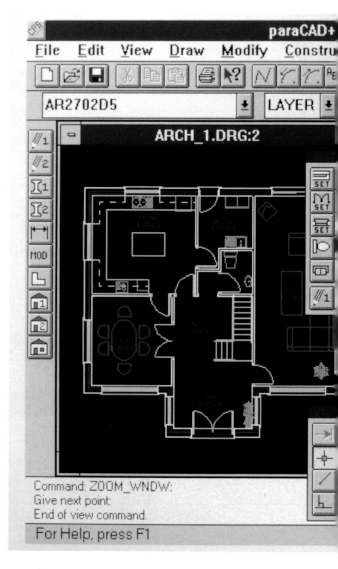

A typical screen (in this case from paraCAD+, a 2D drafting program) showing the command line, drafting areas, and toolbars

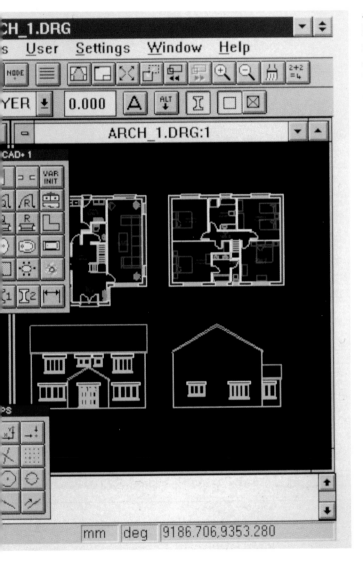

atoms, in making programs present a similar iconic face to the world as traditional media. But this common platform has the advantage for the user that the initial learning cycle on a new program is quite a rapid one, since the user does not have to learn a new menu structure or sequences of command keystrokes to begin operating a program. While there is not yet complete uniformity, for example in the way commands are displayed as icons, the convention of menus, toolbars and dialog boxes is generally parallel. But this superficial resemblance does not mean that all programs execute the same function in the same way, or that all programs perform the same tasks with equal rapidity and ease. The algorithms applied by different programs in carrying out similar operations are not necessarily the same.

2D CAD

The first screen on a program normally looks something like the one shown on the preceding page. Along the top of the screen is the file name, with standard buttons to increase or decrease screen size and to exit or switch from the program. Beneath them are the main command menus (file, edit, draw, symbol, modify, snaps, zoom, help) each of which has a pull-down menu of further commands. Below these is a selection of icons for common functions (open a file, save a file, rotate, zoom in, zoom out, etc.). Down the left-hand edge is the toolbox with its individual buttons for selecting objects, for drawings lines, rectangles and curves, for writing text lines and for creating layers. At the bottom of the screen is an information line, showing which command, button or icon has been selected, the position of the cursor on the page and the grid scale. The rest of the screen is the drawing area. A mouse (or other pointing tool such as a light pen) is used both to click on the commands and to make the appropriate marks on the drawing area, which is divided into a grid. Not all programs will organize the screen in the same way, but the same elements are often present.

Imagine that you wanted to draw a plan for a trade fair stand. Choosing the drawing tool would allow you to set out the outlines, either in straight lines or curves. Further elements can be added (bézier curves are used to mark out individual meeting areas, superimposed squares a display unit) and standard items can be drawn from a library of standard elements (chairs, doors, windows, and so on). Objects in the drawings (lines

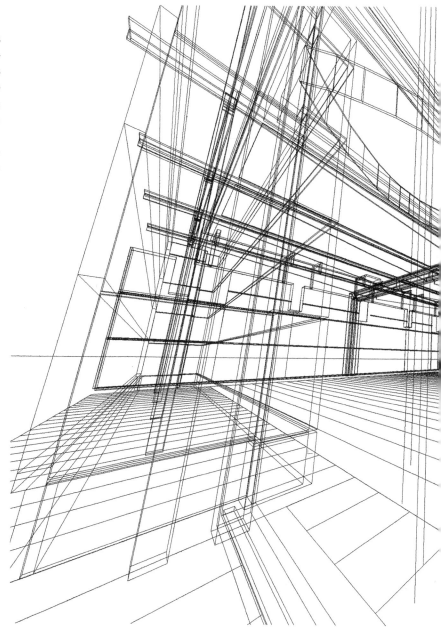

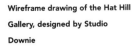

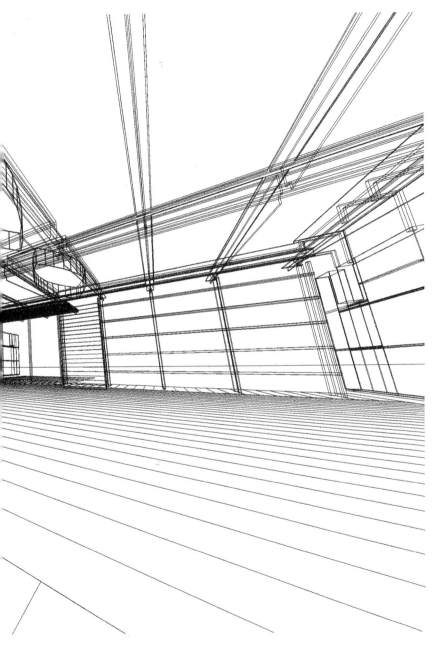

or groups of lines or symbols) can be scaled, different layers can be added for different levels of information, and measurements between selected points can be added. Hatching according to selected patterns can be applied to differentiate between functions. In this way an entry-level 2D CAD programme can be used to create quite sophisticated drawings.

Wireframe

Wireframe drawing is the ancestor of contemporary CAD presentation (Ivan Sutherland, whom many hail as the inventor of Virtual Reality, used wireframe drawings for his flight simulator). But the technique of wireframe is still a valuable first stage in establishing the skeleton of the building, and is the starting point for many 2D and 3D CAD programs. AutoCAD, for example, offers the option of assembling an initial drawing in 2D, and in 3D either as an axonometric or in perspective. To create an axonometric drawing the grid lines are simply set at the required angle to generate an axonometric form.

Wireframe drawing can also be used creatively as a presentation tool. For the Goodwood Sculpture Centre at Hat Hill, in southern England, the architect Craig Downie used wireframe drawings to generate the primary design from his paper sketches. 'I don't think I could ever give up using pencil on paper as a way of getting ideas to flow', he explains, 'and perhaps for that reason I like the idea of presenting preliminary projects as wireframe drawings.' These are often generated from odd or even impossible perspectives, and often the hide routines are omitted, so that the whole pattern of lines on the drawing appears.

'For Hat Hill we used both wireframe and rendered views. The first wireframes can be difficult for a client to understand, but once the client did begin to read the drawings they gave him a better understanding of how the parts of the building interrelated and how the design concept was carried through. So the abstract nature of the wireframe drawings actually helped us to develop the project with the client. But because the main building, which serves as an information and exhibition centre for a permanent display of sculpture in the surrounding landscape, was to be set in protected woodland, we needed to produce very clear and realistic images for the planning authority, whose main concern was that the new construction did not damage or degrade the landscape they were, in part, charged with protecting. So here fully rendered images were extremely useful.'

Wireframe drawings also enable an architect to check the 'buildability' of a project from an early stage, since they will inevitably reveal the underlying structure. In terms of designing individual buildings, wireframe is likely to remain a basic tool in the development stages of design.

3D to animation

2D drawings only contain graphical information on a flat plane: plans and elevations, for example, may have to be drawn separately, and are not necessarily related to each other by the program. But they can, depending on the software, be exported to 3D programs

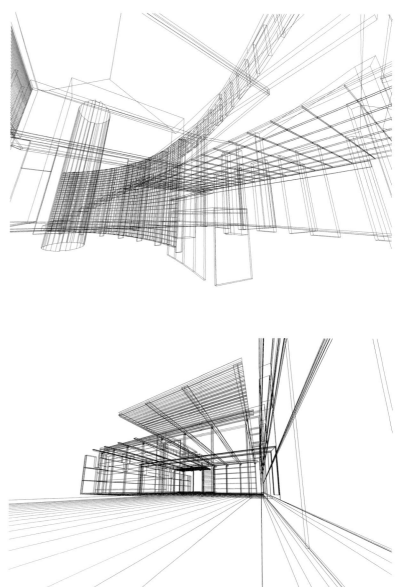

Two wireframe projections of the Hat Hill Gallery

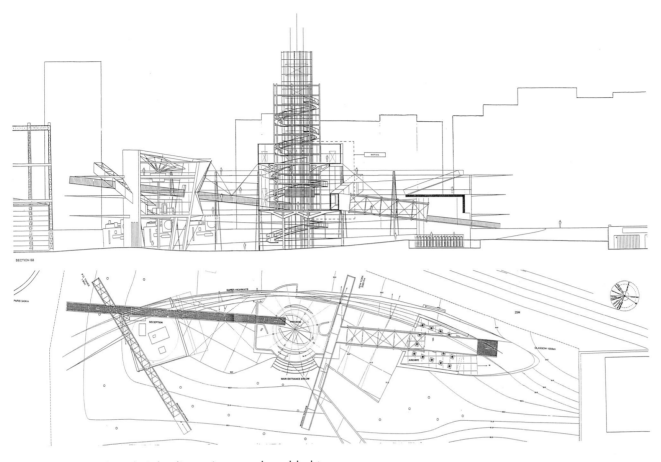

SECTION BB

where height dimensions can be added to the plan, or the two drawings integrated into a three-dimensional space. So perspective views can be generated. This was the approach used by Stuart Rand Bell, in a student project for a site at King's Cross, in London, an area, formerly storage for railway coal and for shunting yards, which has been derelict for some time, but is near both mainline and underground railway services. The new British Library building is nearby. The scheme, entitled a Convergence Centre, was done as part of a final year college project.

'Firstly I made the usual site investigations, taking photographs for reference, paying special attention to the rear of King's Cross station and the nearby gasometers. There

Plan & section of Stuart Rand Bell's Convergence Centre project

was no building specified in the brief for the scheme, just a site. I chose to create *A Primary Terminal to Europe's Communication Networks*. This would be a space where the sole aim would be to receive, process, store and transmit information. It is not the physical contents which are important, unlike the nearby British Library, as hardware can and will be replaced regularly. What was important was the invisible digital information to be held and handled inside the building. The source of ideas for the architectural form was this interplay between visible, irrelevant hardware and invisible, important information. This in turn has a relationship to the ambiguous bulk and transparency of the gasometers, buildings given substance by being filled with invisible gas. So, just like the railway stations nearby this building would be a station for the superhighways of the future.

'The scheme was initially designed on a traditional drawing board using material from various sources and in particular the directional influences of other important information centres. A very simple cardboard model was also made. An ordinance survey plan of the site levels was scanned into the computer and the drawing board sketches and the cardboard model were turned into traditional plans, sections and elevations on the computer (using the program MiniCAD).

A contour map of the site and surrounding areas was made by tracing each contour from the ordinance survey map and giving it a height measurement. The rings of the gasometers were traced off the map and given a height estimated from the photographs. These were then duplicated verti-

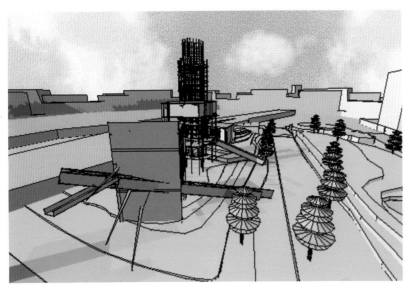

cally and the supporting columns were added to a height shown on the plan.

A block computer model was then made to look at the massing. Various changes were then made to the design, a process lasting about three months. Once the design was fixed the 2D plans, sections and elevations were fixed on the computer, using a carefully planned layering system. The main advantages of using a computer for 2D drawing are ease of correction and the ease of changing scale, though you have to be wary of line weights: the machine doesn't necessarily adjust line weight to the scale you are using, meaning that a change made to a detail you have zoomed in on may appear too heavy once you pull back to the full drawing.

The preliminary 3D model was made by selecting plans of objects and giving them an height. This was done by breaking objects down into elements of walls, floors, ceilings etc. The software used does not allow for transparent or reflective objects, so windows are just holes. Objects were grouped and layered according to relationships to each other. This means that whilst working on one building you don't have to wait for all the others to re draw and also helps with the colouring of objects.

The plans, elevations and existing 3D model were then exported as Drawing Format Exchange (.dfx) files. They were then imported to a second CAD system, Modelshop, in this case, which enables shadow effects and animation sequences to be generated, but which is not so capable as a 2D drafting tool.

'To create the skyline a number of building silhouettes were placed in the distance at the approximate height of surrounding buildings. Up to this point everything was drawn as a wireframe. Occasionally it was useful to set up one or two key views and render them at a low quality setting or without all the layers visible, to begin to build up an impression of how the final building would look. To create the appearance of the sky itself I took a photograph in my back garden and scanned it into the computer. This was then inserted as a background picture. You may notice that it does not change as the views change, but hopefully your attention is never on the sky!

'When creating an animation it is often useful to make the movement of the virtual camera into a complete loop, so that you come back to where you started, so that the viewer is always seeing the building moving in the same direction, and can establish an orientation. Various views were taken from around the site. Each view was established by selecting a point on the plan to look from and then the height at which the observer is above the ground was also fixed. As the ground was also contoured, I had to add on the height of the contour too. I then selected a point on the plan towards which the observer is looking, and then indicated the height of that point. If the second point is higher than the first then the viewer will obviously be looking upwards. I could also set the perspective to various settings, depending upon how realistic I wanted the view to be. The views were then set to a low resolution setting for testing.

Three renderings of a new building in Docklands by Pawson Williams, London

'The next step was to try out a simple animation. It was necessary to define the order of the views and the number of frames between each view. For the first run I kept the number of frames to about 10. The computer then worked out the additional views needed for an animation. This showed me whether the video would clip the edges of buildings or go beneath ground level, neither of which were desirable in this case. Once I was happy with the first rough, it was time to re-select each view and improve the quality setting to include a higher screen resolution and the addition of shadows. The number of frames between each view was therefore increased to 40, giving more realistic motion. Then the computer renders each frame and can either create a small file for each view or one large one for all of them. As I had about 400 frames I selected small files as this is less likely to cause problems later, especially if the video was to be re-edited. During the creation of the animation I would normally leave the machine to get on with it. Once all the files have been made a viewing program puts all the frames in to sequence and packs them together into one file for viewing or distribution.'

Solid Modelling

But just as some architects prefer to develop initial designs with pencil and paper, others prefer handling and placing three-dimensional objects such as blocks of wood or foam. This is particularly valuable where an arrangement of buildings is being planned, and where their relationship with each other is as important, in the initial stage, as the detailed appearance of the individual buildings. Solid modelling programs come into their own here, as they enable the architect to move rapidly to a set of 'building blocks' which can be manipulated as discrete objects on screen. Keith Williams of Pawson Williams Architects finds that this is their preferred technique. 'This immediate 3D visual quality is a most important aspect in developing the design at its earliest stages: the importance of the computer is as an interface between the physical design and the abstract ideas behind it. In other words we are interested in CAD as an architectural tool, not as a tool for building. It is a way of

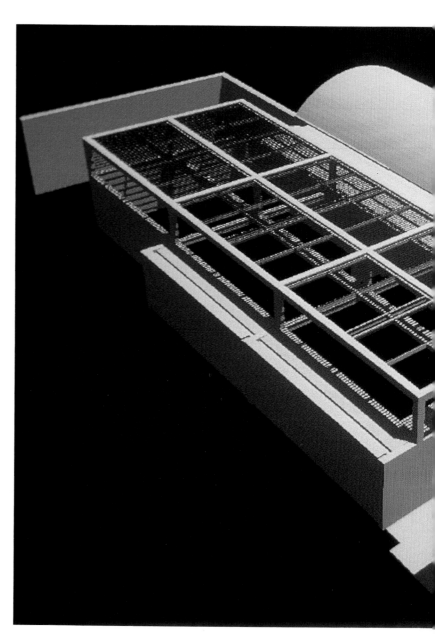

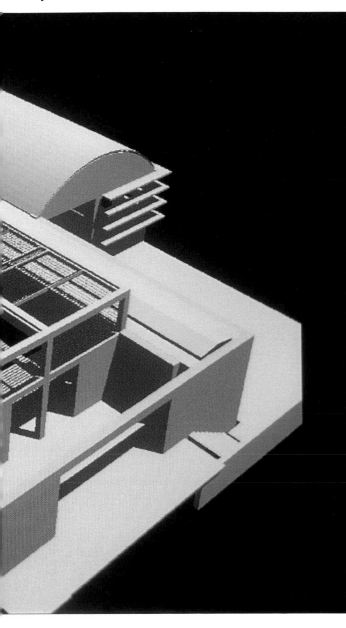

View of the Dover Castle visitor centre,
by Pawson Williams

codifying a design process that makes the drawing real in itself, and is more important than its representation of visual aspects,' he explains, 'we'd shy away from using an engineering-based package, for example, at too early a stage in the design process, since we would find it too restricting, particularly as we prefer to work conceptually with our engineers at the outset.'

And because it is an abstract design process, in the early stage, realistic colour rendering can be as much a hindrance as a help. In these proposals for an office building in London's Docklands (pp. 38-39), there was no need to make the structural colour correct, as the key problem was the proportional relationship of the main forms. 'For a visitor's centre at Dover, however, which was deliberately to be built of wood - something we decided at an early stage given the brief and the site - we rendered the model in a wood colour and finish at an early stage.' Pawson Williams' work highlights one of the inherent contradictions in realistic modelling. A design, Terry Pawson points out, is but one version of the concept of a building, and the finished building is another version. There are sequential and logical links between them, but they are both subsets of the main 'ideal building'.

The proposal for a World's Fair in Budapest has also been modelled in abstract colours, to emphasize the relationships between the buildings and the functionality of the fair site. Here again, realism is not the main issue (particularly since the individual pavilions will be designed and built by the participating countries). What is important, and what a solid modelled image helps to understand, is the underlying rationale of the scheme.

Realistic Modelling

At a later stage in the design process, however, realistic models come into their own. They are increasingly essential to ensure the smooth passage of a project through planning and approval, and to communicate with clients, particularly if the client is a large organization where not all staff will have the ability to read the information relevant

41

to them from plans and elevations.

In the case of a new building in central London, architects, clients and planners were concerned that the scale and proportions of the whole should merge well with the surrounding historic buildings, and in particular that the roofline of the new building would fit in with the surrounding roofscape. The images were created by Richard Garton by importing the main plans and elevations as .dxf files into 3D Studio. Here fully three-dimensional images were created, and then rendered in the appropriate colours and with atmospheric lighting. A flyaround was then created from a series of individual images from different perspective positions, which were then animated into a complete video sequence at 25 frames per second. Finally, Adobe Photoshop was used to create a series of montages which helped to show diagramatically the relationship of the new building with its future surroundings, and these were edited, with a soundtrack, into the video.

The different levels of design complexity that can be achieved by different programs or combinations of programs represent tools for different parts of the architect's task, rather than a hierarchy of programs that has to be scaled. The importance of the development of CAD systems for architecture is that they offer architects choice in how to approach design and presentation tasks. The systems are enabling, not obligatory. If CAD can make part of the architect's task less tiresome or time-consuming, or can help the client better understand a design, then it has value.

Two video views of a new development in central London

program

The Autodesk adventure

The Autodesk adventure

One convenient starting point for telling the story of Autodesk is January 30th, 1982. On that Saturday afternoon John Walker sat down at his home in Marin County, California, with an informal group of friends and associates to discuss the creation of a new software company. Fifteen years later the company they set about cobbling together is Autodesk Inc., currently worth around a billion dollars, and the creators of the industry standard computer-aided design package for PCs, AutoCAD.

John Walker and Dan Drake had been running Marinchip Systems for two years. With a number of partners they had built up a reasonable business supplying software and boards for a number of different processors. However, Walker felt that this was going nowhere, for two reasons. Firstly, the margins for a small company producing both hardware and software were too narrow, and, secondly, the arrival of new personal computers was bound to change the market radically. Walker felt the way forward was to concentrate entirely on software. They would identify market areas for new products where their skills as programmers could be used to best effect. Walker's invitation to join him also embraced a wider perception: that computing as a whole, by moving onto the desktop, would change from the preserve of 'techies' to a general business tool, and that the attitudes that had served in the past would also have to change. In the agenda for the first meeting he suggests 'don't expect MSP (the proposed company) to be as much fun as hacking; do expect MSP to educate you in the realities of business, and make you rich.' He was saying to his colleagues - a group 'with the technical competence edge on almost everybody' - that it was time, in a

The founding members of Autodesk

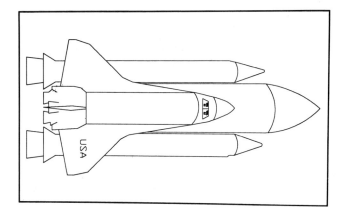

Two drawings produced to promote

early releases of AutoCAD

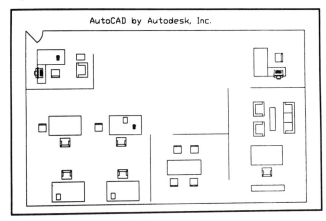

sense, to grow up, even though the company structure and system of remuneration and rewards proposed was as freewheeling and evenhanded as possible.

Autodesk was founded by sixteen people, most of them already employed full-time in computing in the San Francisco Bay area. Their commitment to MSP was to put an agreed portion of their other time at the company's disposal in developing an agreed range of products. The company was to be run on minimal costs, with the return to the founders as much in additional stock options as in money until the company was up and running. The regular letters and circulars, mainly by John Walker, from the early years of the company, have been published as *The Autodesk Files* (New Riders Publishing, California, 1989). They make an intoxicating mixture of exhortation, ruthless business sense, reflections on the arcana of Californian tax law, detailed programming comments and literary allusions from Kropotkin to Neil Young.

The company was formally incorporated in April 1982. As it did not ship its first products until the end of that year, the first year was loss making, but thereafter profits and sales rose at an astonishing rate. By 1985, when the company went public, raising $10 million on the stock market, sales were over $27 million. The value of the original investors' $1 dollar shares was the equivalent of $165 dollars. By 1988 sales were $117 million, and by 1994 $465 million. The company has an enviable reputation for the quality of its programming, and its ability to innovate. In tune with its open approach to solving problems, John Walker, who had guided the fortunes of the company for the first six years, retired from the chairmanship in 1988 to devote himself to full-time programming.

Walker was right, in 1982, to see that the particular moment was the right one for a new software venture, with the expansion of computing facilities not matched by the then available software. One of the first lists of potential products includes a cardfile programme for organizing 'the things you currently keep on scraps of paper': a key aspect of this was that it would require 'absolutely no knowledge other than how to turn on the computer and type,' a program for generating and filling business forms either for a database or for printing out, an executive planning aid for resource allocation and costings in large businesses, and - perhaps prophetically - a screen editor to be called Window ('probably no market, damned shame')! The cardfile was renamed Autodesk, after which the company was also named, though the product prototype was never brought to the market. Another product ripe for development was Interact, a graphics program, which Mike Riddle, one of the founders, had already been developing, and which Walker called 'a superb product in a virgin market', even if its memory requirements included the then-unusual feature of a hard disk.

Interact was the product that was in due course to become AutoCAD. The prototypes were demonstrated at the West Coast Computer Faire and the COMDEX exhibition in 1982, and the first version, AutoCAD 80 was officially released in December 1982. AutoCAD 86, the version for the new IBM PC, was released in January 1983. The product has been regularly updated to add new features, and a large family of subsidiary programs have ben developed for special functions by Autodesk and others. AutoCAD is the current market leader for computer-aided design, with over 1 million units in use worldwide, both in architects' offices and in engineering and design companies.

The success of AutoCAD can be dated back to Walker's original perception that graphic

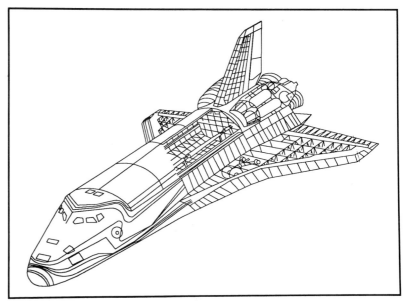

Two drawings created in Auto-CAD 86 by Sean O'Donnell (*above*) and Duff Kurland (*facing*) show the increasing sophistication of the program

48

drafting on screen did not need to be the preserve of dedicated workstations and programs, but could, through skilful programming, be made available on a PC, and for a price of 1,000 dollars, compared to the ten thousand dollar price tag of other programs. This logic is today self-evident, but in 1982 there was a widespread view that nothing new could be done with the computer. Walker and his colleagues refusal to accept that view was at the heart of Autodesk. History has proved them absolutely right.

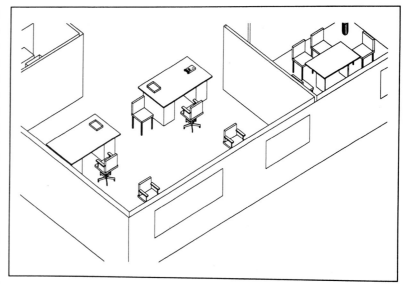

But Walker's opinion was not merely based on his extraordinary ability as a programmer, but on a wider perception of the computer as a tool that was no longer to be the preserve of the specialist but should be usable by all comers. In addition, he realized that computer-aided design was not just a tool for use by architects and engineers, or even just a tool for anybody who needed to draw as part of their work or activity. It was also symbolical of the power of the computer to model the real world. In other words, a true CAD program would be 'a system which describes physical objects, and knows about the various ways in which they interact (and can be taught about interactions as we define new forms of geometry today)', as Walker wrote in a 1986 paper entitled 'Computer Aided Design: vertical market application, general purpose productivity tool, or the heart of computer science?'

At about the same time Walker announced that Autodesk would be making a major investment in Ted Nelson's Xanadu project. Xanadu was named after the 'stately pleasure dome' in Samuel Taylor Coleridge's poem, *Kublai Khan* describing 'a treasure-house of rare device', a realm in which all the riches of the world were stored. It was also the title given to Citizen Kane's monstrous palace in Orson Welles's film, which many believe took as its central metaphor the life of Randolph Hearst and his castle at San Simeon. The poem also plays a role in Douglas Adams' brilliantly funny novel *Dirk Gently's Holistic Detective Agency,* and the writer Angus Wilson used as a title for his collected essays *A Person from Porlock* (the poet was interrupted during its composition by a 'person from Porlock' visiting him and driving the vision of Xanadu from his mind).

For Ted Nelson the riches of his Xanadu were a metaphor for knowledge, for Xanadu was to be an immense electronic library cum database. Users would access documents via their computers, using a modem and a telephone line, paying an access fee, and could deposit their own documents there, which would also earn fees if accessed by other users. But the fee aspect was only intended to cover the running costs of the program. Its radical intent was to make knowledge as freely available as possible, and to change radically the conventional publishing process, which limits the print-runs of books and restricts access to the market to those authors judged financially viable by publishers.

The information in the documents would also be interconnected via a database, so that the query *Xanadu* would call up the poem, the film, the novel and the book of essays, and direct the reader to biographies of Coleridge and Welles and to the other

Stills from Orson Welles' 1941 film
Citizen Kane, **showing the palace of**
Xanadu

50

writings of Ted Nelson, Douglas Adams and Angus Wilson. It would reach further, depending on the completeness of the database, into Eric Linklater's comic novel in which the hero's grandfather is the 'person from Porlock', into *Purchas his Pilgrimes*, an anonymous early book of travels in which Xanadu is first described, and so on. Access and interrelationships were at the heart of Nelson's idea.

The Xanadu project has still to mature. But just as Coleridge's poem is also famous for being unfinished, the concept itself of Xanadu has had an immense influence on the development and philosophy of the Internet. On the Net the principles of free access to all sites, of freedom to publish whatever material on the Net, and to contact other users at will are basic tenets. The story of the Internet is not strictly relevant to this story of computer-aided design, and, like Heraclitus' river, it is changing and moving so fast that stepping into it even once is probably impossible. But in passing it is worth noting that there are user groups on the Net for many of the main CAD programs, and that most software manufacturers have pages on the World Wide Web with product information and updates, and support services for users.

In 1994 the radical architectural publishers Princeton Architectural Press announced Architecture on Line, an independent bulletin board on their own server which gives architects and architectural writers free space to public reviews, essays and comments. And the London architectural publishers Ellipsis in spring 1995 published their guide to contemporary architecture in Tokyo on the Net before publishing the conventional printed edition. With the announcement of publicly available software that is intended to set a standard for viewing 3D images on the World Wide Web the possibility that architects will be able to take even more advantage of the Net extends considerably.

The current language for text and designs on the Web and the Net is HTML, or Hyper Text Markup Language, which does provide links to graphics created in various other formats. Silicon Graphics in California has announced their new

Orson Welles as Citizen Kane,

in the halls of Xanadu

VRML - Virtual Reality Markup Language - will be available for free, and can be used to create readable files of three dimensional images.

Autodesk also took a stake in the Virtual Reality market with their announcement in 1989 of the Cyberia project, intended to create a set of software tools for designing objects and spaces in Virtual Reality. These could be used in the entertainments business, in engineering design and in architecture. But John Walker saw the potential of cyberspace in wider terms. It is 'a general purpose of technology of interaction with computers,' he wrote in a paper *Through the Looking Glass* in 1988. 'New technologies tend to be initially applied in the most obvious and literal ways. When graphic displays were first developed, they were used for obvious graphics applications... Only later did people come to see that appropriate use of two dimensional graphics could help clarify even exclusively text or number oriented tasks. So it will be with cyberspace. Cyberspace represents the first three dimensional computer interface worthy of the name.'

In 1995 Autodesk released version 5.0 of AutoCAD AEC, a program that shows how this goal set out by John Walker of modelling the real world is being approached. The inclusion in release 5 of AutoCAD AEC of a first generation of objects is very relevant. This program joins in the Autodesk stable AutoCAD release 14, the three dimensional version of the original AutoCAD programme, now available in both DOS and Windows versions, and 3D Studio, a complete rendering program which also allows the user to create video sequences and fly-throughs. The importance of the object routines in AutoCAD AEC was explained by David Clarke, who trained as an architect and is now in charge, with the programmer Simon Jones, of developing AutoCAD AEC from Autodesk's UK office.

'In terms of moving our programs into object-based ones, the current releases of AutoCAD and AutoCAD AEC have the facility to create objects, and we are building up a set of common definitions for aspects of objects. These are

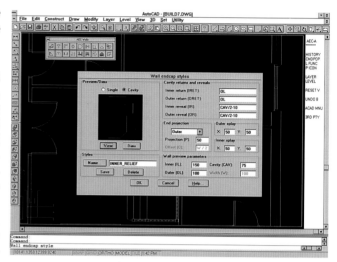

The three screen shots on these pages show how AutoCAD AEC 5 uses the screen interface to help the design process

not only available to third party developers, but will also be put into the public domain: we are working with government agencies and the European Union on a three year project to do this. Making the basic definitions for objects non-proprietary in this way is of course heresy in traditional programming terms, but I believe it is necessary for the future, which must lie in open sharing of data.

'At present AutoCAD AEC 5 has what I would call prototype objects in it: we aim to have complete interoperability in due course. By that I mean that files, objects or documents compiled under any software can be easily imported into any other. And these imported items can appear either as visual items in a graphic display, or as information.'

'If we could write the rules and definitions for objects first, programming them would be no problem. But in practice it doesn't and can't work that way. A program is never set in stone: we have sent out a first version as a starting point, and with the feedback from users we will gradually develop a more and more complete set of rules.

'AutoCAD policy is to break the links, end the myths and legends, and make things affordable for everybody, to create programs that are flexible, adaptable and cheap: when you consider that 90 percent of the construction industry consists of firms with fewer than 20 employees, that is a mass market, not able to afford an expensive dedicated system. Eight years ago when I joined Autodesk, a 2D program that could perform tasks such as drawing walls automatically

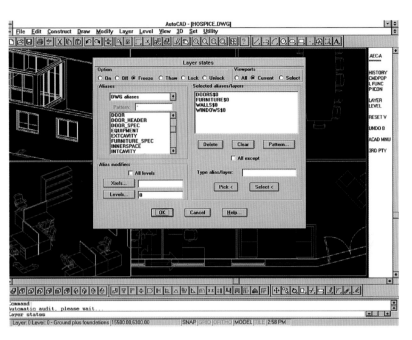

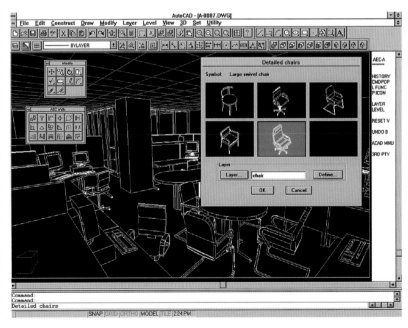

was quite revolutionary, and in a small practice it cut a tremendous amount of workload. Other big system programs were offering 3D design and solid modelling, but they cost a great deal and required large memories and extensive computing power. Our problem then was to get people away from the drawing board and onto the computer. Now, eight years later, is the right time to be looking at 3D once the 2D drafting problems have been solved.

'One thing we set out to do was to destroy the fog of jargon surrounding computing. This jargon was confusing - even conning - a lot of people, and we wanted to blow that away, along with the 'computers are going to take over attitude': our basic premise was the computer as a tool, operated by a pen or a mouse that was connected to a human arm and controlled by a human brain. The computer is there to free up the architect's time for the important work to be done.

'Putting the architect in charge means looking at the architect's requirements first. Our user group meetings are constructively controversial, to develop these personal links. What I keep saying to them is that CAD vendors don't control what goes into the software, you, the users, do. Often a programmer sits in on the meetings and writes the new code with the meeting, to make sure it meets the users' needs. In any new release of AEC, we reckon that sixty percent of the updates meet the users perceived requirements at that date, and the other forty percent are what we think they are going to need over the next twelve months, that being the usual interval between upgrades. Today the main market can only be called extremely sophisticated: it understands the technology and what it can do for them. They are now looking for 3D intelligent modelling. There has been a lot of important academic work on this over the last few years, and what we are doing is bringing this into practical use. After all, we believe in evolutionary rather than revolutionary design. For example, an intelligent object needs structure: so we have been providing a structuring system through the layering facility from the beginning. Another problem is data exchange. In the past architects have felt it was sufficient to send in the plans on paper to the client, and stop there. But increasingly information is being handled electronically, not on paper, and the client needs the complete information set not only for the design stage and then for construction, but also for the continued management of the building after completion. So now it is the clients who are pushing for these developments to happen.'

We took the opportunity to ask David Clarke about the Cyberia project. The original directors of the program left after a year or so, and little has been heard of it in the meantime. He is convinced of the importance of Virtual Reality to the architecture industry. 'At present, VR is only at a visualization level - in which it is making great progress. But you can't have what I might call 'professional' virtual reality without an intelligent system, and so the next development will be to create VR systems that can handle objects, so that you can not only explore the visual space but also manipulate data. There would be no point in using a VR system to study a projected building if you couldn't see all the consequences of changes. Not just the appearance aspects,

Two views of an office building, created in AutoCAD AEC then imported into 3D Studio for rendering

but how changes would affect the building programme, the costings, and so on. We are already working with various specialists in the VR field, so that when our objects software is fully developed the VR applications will be ready and waiting for them. Again, we have about a three-year timescale for this.

'These new technologies are going to give us - thinking of myself as an architect - the opportunity to get right back into the central heart of creating both designs and buildings. With an object-based system, this means that whoever designs the first object in a project sits at the centre of the process. Now this means the architect has got to invest in the right software - with a cheap 2D system that can't communicate with anything else it will be back to recession! But a number of architects have been finding that in a changing marketplace the right system is an asset. Architects are moving into providing facilities management services, for example in the health service.

'We have generated a lot of thinking within the construction industry: just as they are driving us to the leading edge we are trying to push them there as well. Achieving this means beginning with reliable systems and systems support. One of our user groups has a team working on a proposal for the architect's office of the year 2005, which we see as being completely online, not only for graphics but for all paperwork. It has been said that computing is no longer an act of faith, it's a necessity to run a business: I believe that is absolutely true for architecture, today and tomorrow.'

David Clarke approaches the future of computing in architecture and construction from a realistic standpoint, mixed with considerable humour (the code-name for one program at an early stage of its development was Basingstoke, the name of a wholly undistinguished town in southern England, 'because there's not a lot going on there.' With one of his user groups he also produced a semi-spoof video, with architect and developer discussing the cost per user effectiveness of Carrara marble floors for a cruciform shopping mall, in a wine bar entitled Rogues. The video neatly conveys the value of Autodesk products in presentation and design terms, while quietly poking fun at some of the pretensions of the profession.

The mixture of pragmatism and idealism that runs through the story of the early years of Autodesk may have been transmuted into solid business sense as the company grew to be the fifth largest software company in the world. But the central essence is still there. John Walker's view that 'when you're interacting with a computer you are not conversing with another person, you are exploring another world' is being given concrete form through programs that can handle intelligent objects, that can import and export files and data across different programs and platforms, and which seek to extend itself not monolithically but by encouraging third-party developers and creating public domain standards.

57

Surfing the data stream

Surfing the data stream

Autodesk set about creating tools for designers based on graphics, enabling them to plot future designs on screen. This ability to visualize is a key part of the design process, especially in the creative stage, but almost immediately a large number of other considerations, not purely visual, come into play. What material will the design be in, what functions will it have to perform, how will it be constructed, how much will it cost, and so on. Architects and engineers have a 'trained intuition' that allows them to deal with such questions on an ad hoc basis while beginning the design process, so that their attention is not endlessly deflected into side issues. But in complex projects organizing the analysis of an evolving design is a major task.

George Stevenson and his colleagues at Engineering Technology, based in Derby, England, started in 1979 to look at the design and planning process in the construction industry. Stevenson realized that the process of tendering for parts of a building contract was, for the contractors, a time-consuming process, in which each contractor went through the same tasks. By creating a database of available electrical fittings and making it generally available to the industry, a lot of current duplication of effort could be avoided. In addition the software to access the database contained installation labour time standards, so that both elements of costing, materials and labour, were available. A price-updating service was also included. This database was released in 1983, for electrical services, and was followed in 1985 by one for mechanical services. Since then both databases have been donated to the industry, and become industry standards in the UK.

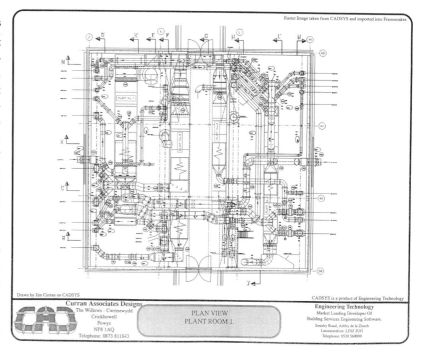

Raster Image taken from CADSYS and imported into Framemaker.

Drawn by Jim Curran on CADSYS

Curran Associates Designs
The Willows - Cwrtnewydd
Crickhowell
Powys
NP8 1AQ
Telephone: 0873 811843

PLAN VIEW
PLANT ROOM 1.

CADSYS is a product of Engineering Technology

Engineering Technology
Market Leading Developer Of
Building Services Engineering Software.
Smisby Road, Ashby de la Zouch
Leicestershire. LE65 2UU
Telephone: 0530 560000

CADSYS is a program for assembling and linking elements in a design. It is particularly useful for HVAC and electrical installations. The plan (*above*), perspective and isometric views (*facing*) of a hospital heating plant room were created in CADSYS and then exported to Framemaker for output, by Curran Associates Designs in Wales

Engineering Technology also worked on maintenance management systems for contracted-out building services maintenance. Here again the system was promoted to encourage standard maintenance specifications across the industry. From the question of industry standards Stevenson and others then started looking at ways in which design, estimating, contracting, construction and maintenance can be integrated, using computer-aided design and relational databases.

The main problem here was not so much a technical one as an organizational one, even a cultural one. The construction industry is anything but a monolith. On a major project there could well be seven or eight independent partners working for the same client - surveyors, civil engineers, architects, steel fabricators, electrical and plumbing and air conditioning contractors, builders, and so on. Each of these independent disciplines has its own design principles, working methods, and conventions. Their contractual rules and practices differ, as does the software they are increasingly using in the planning and design stages.

The major problem lay - and still lies - in the network of interlacing responsibilities endemic in a complex building contract. Delay and additional costs are always a risk, and each contracting party seeks to limit its individual responsibility for paying such costs. A cynic might compare such a situation to the children's game of passing the parcel, in which the blame for any cost overruns is pushed from one party to another. Persuading the construction industry to put such frankly adversarial attitudes aside is a difficult but necessary task. The same situation had been found in parts of manufacturing industry in the UK in the 1960s and 1970s. There demarcation disputes and outdated trade practices on the shop floor combined with a management obsession with price rather than cost effectively destroyed a number of major businesses. This has been aptly described as 'a completely crazy situation, in which success depended on the ability to pass liability to someone else in the chain.' The alternative procedure in the construction business was to overload one's fellow contractors with raw information - revised plans, updated schedules, new detail drawings, whether relevant or not to any mutual tasks, so as to be

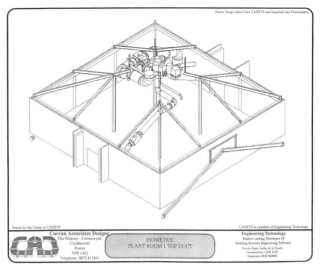

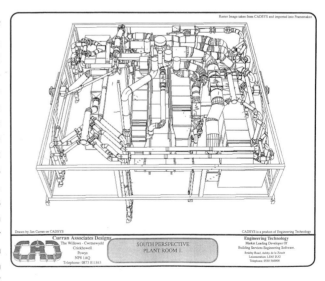

well covered in case of a dispute. This flow of information between the different parties is of course a necessity: but for the job to proceed efficiently it needs to be an organized flow, in which the consequences of changes in one area can be redlined through to the other areas involved.

To take a simple example, suppose the size of the windows on one floor of an office building is changed by the client. The architect produces a new drawing, the glazing contractor a revised specification. But the consequences do not stop there: changing the window area also changes the load on the heating, ventilation and air conditioning system. If more ductwork is required, then that will have to be integrated into the ceiling plan, and if the new ductwork will not fit into the space of the old, then changes will have to be made to the other systems (electrical, telephone, data, fire protection) running through the same space. If the change requires a modification to the boiler-room, then the car parking plan in the rest of the basement needs to be modified, and so on. A simple aesthetic modification can run through many other aspects of a complex structure.

Everyone in the construction industry - clients and contractors - knows that delays, design conflicts and cost changes occur on almost every complex project. But the adversarial nature of the tendering and contract system has tended to prevent an open discussion of this. No single contractor wants to break ranks and tell the client that problems are likely to occur. One possible approach to this difficulty was to offer the cli-

Sonata used to map structural elements in two buildings. Note the use of colour coding for different features

62

Exterior views: once the basic 3D model
has been assembled it can be viewed in
perspective (*right*), or from a chosen
viewpoint (*above*) while background
effects can be added for greater realism

ent a way of evaluating potential conflicts or bottlenecks at the design stage, and of continuously monitoring design changes in all areas through an integrated model.

To achieve this, designers had to create compatibility between the software systems used by architects and contractors, so that files produced in different systems could be read concurrently into the same model. This was a problem which required considerable programming skills to solve, but was a preferable approach to developing new software for the different tasks and hoping to persuade contractors to adopt it in preference to their own systems. The other task was to develop a CAD system that could correlate all these different files into a coherent whole. Here it was soon found that Sonata, a parametric CAD system in use by large architectural practices, was easily adaptable to the new task: other object-based programs include Reflex, designed by Jonathan Ingram.

A parametric CAD program differs from a traditional program in one key way. In a standard program the design is held in the computer memory as a series of point relationships (in a 2D program) or as groups of pixels (in a 3D or rendering program). In a parametric program the visual information is part of a database of information: it is one representation of the data relating to the on-screen item. Consider a door. In a 2D program, the doorframe is a set of four coordinates at parallel paired distances. These may have been drawn by the architect, or imported from a library of standard images: either way in terms of information, they con-

64

Using sequential functions in Sonata to layer the constructional details in an office interior

sist of coordinates plus a label. The program may be able to count the number of occurrences of the same label in a design: this is a first step towards a true parametric program. In a parametric program each element in the design (door, window, wall-panel, etc.) is an 'object'. As such, the object description is not only its spatial coordinates in plan and elevation, but also whatever other data the architect wishes to enter into the object library, a database linked permanently to the object. In the case of the door, this could include its manufacturer, cost, colour, weight, fire-resistance, locking system, and the date at which it should be delivered and installed. Each similar door in the design is a parallel object, a second (or third or fourth) version of the original, and each occurrence is noted automatically in the database. In short, the contents of a program are not defined by their spatial relationships, but by their defining parameters, whether graphical or functional.

The second element in a complete parametric program is to make the databases relational. In other words the databases within each object can be interlinked, so that changes in one specification either make corresponding changes elsewhere or alert the user to the need to respecify. In the case of changing window sizes mentioned earlier, the relationality would ensure that the ductwork was 'told' of the changed demand, and the list of specified window sizes updated (by the creation of a new object) and so on. At any time the design can be studied either as a visual image, or the databases embedded in each object can be interrogated to provide specific information, just like a traditional alphanumeric database: what is the total cost of the building to this stage, for example, or what is the list of suppliers for different elements, or what is the schedule of deliveries to site. The completed design can be used to create complete schedules of materials, work schedules, even purchase orders.

Such a program gives the architect a degree of control over the building being designed not matched by conventional CAD programs. Sonata and Reflex, among the best para-

metric programs, also have a full range of
conventional drawing, rendering and visualizing tools. Running on a Unix workstation,
they provide some of the highest quality
architectural visualizations around. But for
construction planning this capacity was a
useful bonus only: the value of Sonata or Reflex was that they could accommodate, via
the parametric structure, the additional layers of information from the parallel software
used by contractors. Such programs could
build the model that would allow potential
conflict points to be identified in the early
stages of the design process, and could be
used during the construction phase to check
the validity of design modifications as they
necessarily occur. The model would be the
arbiter of design decisions, and would reduce duplication of design effort, delay and
cost overruns.

Engineering Technology, who use Reflex,
saw that they were well placed to offer this
technology to the construction industry and
to architects, since they were not part of the
construction team, and so could stand aside
from the culture clashes within the industry.
Nor were they seeking to take over control
of the design and building process. Together
with others, they were able to find a major
project, the rebuilding of Smithfield Market
in London, in which the main contractors,
Taylor Woodrow, architects Richard Rogers
& Partners and the property developers
Stanhope agreed to 'test-drive' the system
to see whether it would produce the ben-
efits suggested. It was so successful that it
was adopted for a further major project, the
construction of the Heathrow Express rail
link from London to the airport. The system
is also being used by Richard Rogers & Part-

Drawing out the whole perspective plan of a development in Sonata

ners and the construction company Bovis to control the building of a new terminal at Heathrow Airport for the British Airports Authority.

The Heathrow project showed up one particular advantage of the system. Not only did it allow the modelling and evaluation of a very complex construction process in terms of structure, it also allowed the timing of the different construction phases to be analysed into very tight elements. This was essential in a situation where construction work was taking place in the middle of the busiest airport in Europe, and where the final building would be integrated into the whole surrounding structure. Operational and security considerations between landside and airside were affected by the construction programme, and these could be checked out and adapted into a work schedule on a day by day basis. In this way a project management system not only handled the three dimensions of the physical building, but also the fourth dimension of time.

Since the relational databases that are at the heart of project management programs such as Reflex and Sonata can also carry cost information, the program can be described as truly five dimensional - the three dimensions of space, the fourth of time and the fifth one, cost - being all within the ambit of the program. Reflex, designed by Jonathan Ingram, enables the central model to be ported on screen and in real time to the contracting partners. This development uses the high-bandwidth technology of ISDN telephone lines, which can handle the large amounts of data created by the program in real time.

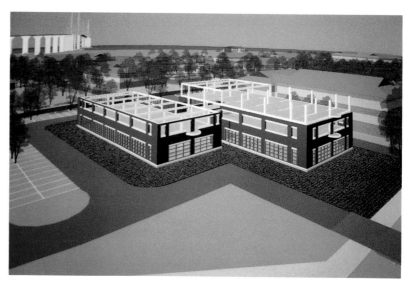

An engineer working on the layout of a sprinkler system, for example, can see that the intended plan conflicts with the positions of beams or ductwork. The engineer can send the plan down the wire to the other parties, and they can see and resolve the problem on screen: changes made in each office are immediately visible on the other parties' screens, with conflict points highlighted. This allows difficulties to be resolved rapidly, without interrupting work on site or involving the different parties in travelling to site meetings or design conferences. It has been suggested that 'with this current technology, and supported by the goodwill of the construction industry, savings of between ten and thirty percent of cost are now feasible.'

Cost savings through project planning enables a 'timed event' model of the project to be produced in which each building element can be time stamped with start and finish dates. Conflicts in the scheduling of construction can be identified and resolved in advance. This development, as Tim Aikin, a developer for Engineering Technology, points out, will allow project planning and design to work in parallel on the same multi-accessible model.

Multi-access modelling is not only useful for developing the construction plan. In the earliest design stage the fact that a model can be accessed by different users will also be a valuable tool for helping clients to develop the initial brief. Every architect knows the situation in which the client knows what is not wanted but does not have a clear idea of what is. Very often design is developed from a list of negative notions ('not too much like this', 'not too much of that') as much as

Once the model is assembled, individual elements can be studied either for phases in construction (*facing*) or for light effects by day and night, for example

69

from a clear positive statement. This is not to suggest that clients do not have a clear vision: simply that the process of stating it is often a difficult one. Any means of improving lines of communication between architect and client at an early stage is valuable.

The graphic designer Neville Brody wrote recently of developments in desktop publishing systems: 'popular access' he pointed out,'redistributes the ability to communicate visually away from the protectionist design industry and gives it back to the original source of the communication.' That architecture should be accessible, not only in terms of the finished building, but also in terms of the design process, is of key importance. If computer aided design systems can empower the client to take part in the design debate, as well as enable the architect to communicate both with the client and a wider public, then architecture in the widest sense will be well served.

Two views of the finished design

Working with Sonata

Working with Sonata

This chapter concentrates on the work of one of the coauthors of this book, Giuliano Zampi. He is a qualified architect trained in the UK and now working in London and Hong Kong. He has specialized in architectural visualizations for several years, regularly winning prizes for his designs in CAD competitions, and exhibiting his work in the architectural section of the Royal Academy Summer Exhibition in London.

His interest is not simply in creating attractive images from architectural drawings, valuable as this process is in communicating the architect's ideas to a client who may not be able to read and understand formal plans and drawings. 'I'm not in the business of offering a finishing service to architects,' he points out. 'My role is as one of the team of consultants on a project, and in some cases I am also the job architect. To execute the original architect's vision involves working alongside the design team from as early a stage as possible: a sophisticated CAD system does allow different options to be reviewed rapidly - for example interior finishes can be revised very easily once the general interior layout is agreed. But much of my work is concerned with technical issues as much as with appearance only.

'In a recent office development in Westminster, for example, we not only modelled the final design in Sonata but also used a time plan to work out the schedule for the building, which contractors would be responsible for which phase. The consequences of changes to the construction plan could also be analysed, and complete schedules of materials generated from the databases. The only access to the site is via busy roads adjoining Westminster Bridge, which was a serious problem. We

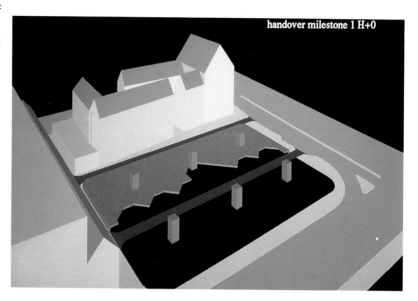

handover milestone 1 H+0

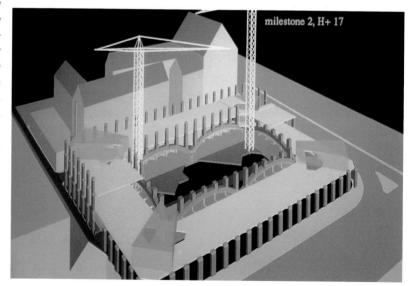

milestone 2, H+ 17

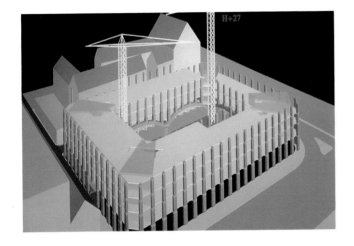

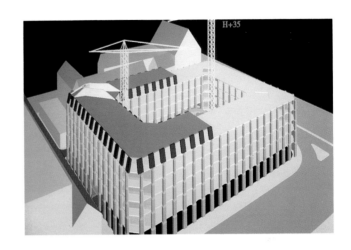

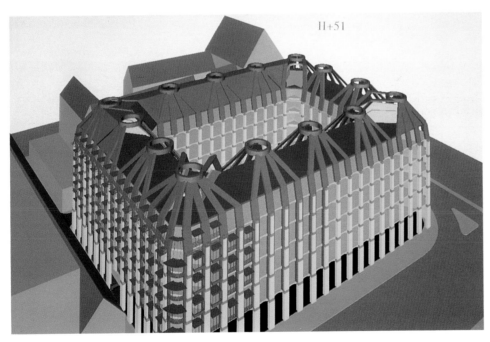

A series of designs showing the construction phases for a new office building in Westminster, London, designed by Michael Hopkins and Partners. Each version of the building is contained within the total design: this is a single object, here viewed in different stages, not a series of designs. Any version (or intermediate stage) can be recalled from the master drawing at any time

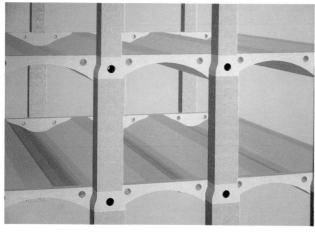

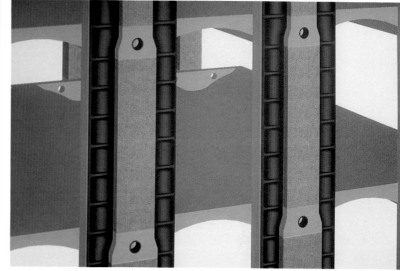

**Five views of the assembly of external
wall elements at Westminster**

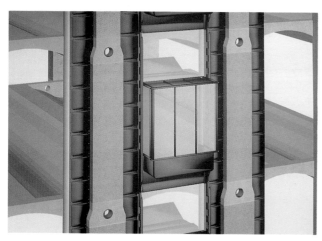

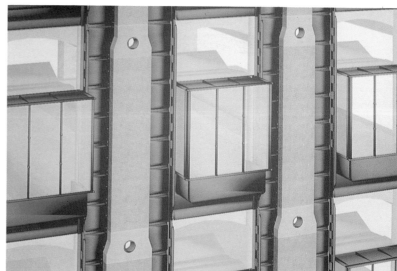

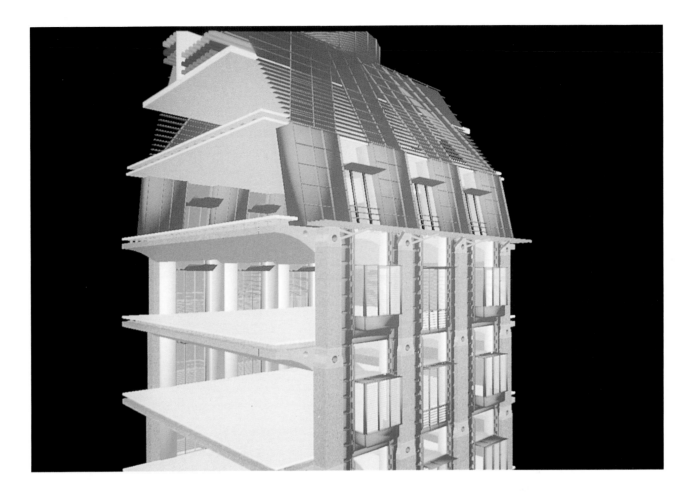

were able to create a critical path analysis for deliveries, so reducing obstructions to a minimum. The interior layout and provision of services, particularly phone and data lines to the individual offices and suites in the building, intended for use by Members of Parliament, was also studied in the on-screen model. In a general office building intended for occupation by a single company this is less of a problem, since the facilities management service will be geared up to regular changes in occupation. Here we knew from the start what the patterns of occupancy were likely to be for a considerable time ahead, but the special requirements of the intended users also meant we had to work very carefully on the interior fitting aspect.

'Lighting, for example, is something that can be detailed technically, but only specialists can read these with confidence. Architects need such systems to check the technical effects lighting will have on the design. This can't be mocked up on hand-built scale models, because you cannot effectively scale lighting sources down to model sizes. I can simulate the effects of lighting on screen, including ranges of lamp colour, and also test alternative lighting schemes very quickly, though this does not produce an exact lighting calculation. Nonetheless this is a powerful tool for architects. In the case of a series of petrol stations, we were concerned with both the visibility of the stations from the highway by day and by night, as well as integrating a new corporate logo and colour scheme into the revised design for the new buildings. Visibility was also an issue from the user's viewpoint: we used the model to ensure that the routes in and out were clear for the drivers both of cars and vans, and that the view from the office and control cabin was adequate both in natural and artificial lighting. A motorist driving along does not want to take too much time looking at a building, particularly at night, to be sure it is a petrol station, so distance studies were also included in our brief.

'The fact that Sonata is an extremely accurate program does not mean that you can only use it for realistic imagery. (In the Westminster project we used realistic colours for the final views, but the same elements in the critical path analysis were colour-coded according to their place in the building plan. This can be achieved using a well-planned database and a sufficiently powerful computer system.) In working with engineers on a new bridge project we deliberately modelled the forms in monochrome on a black background in order to study the formal and technical properties of the design, without being distracted by the intended setting. In this way we can use the program at the purely conceptual phase of design. Because of the additional features in the program, the same model can then be evolved in more realistic ways as the design process advances.

'Just as I can now do more than simply create a plan, section or elevation on computer, so the arrival of high-level programs and the development of multimedia packages that can incorporate moving images and sound into

Three views by night and day of petrol station designs for the Spanish petrol company Repsol, executed in Sonata

a document offer new opportunities. The client brief is all too often a flat compilation of statistics and a few photos to show and explain to the designer the company's profile and image. I would like to see the architect invited to set up an environment or work space on a user-friendly computer system. The client could use this to set a more complete brief for the project, using scanned-in images, text and other media, even music if needed. This information could come from many sources, and would help the architect understand the relative degree of importance of each and every aspect of the brief. Otherwise what tends to happen is that the larger issues in the client's mind, which are difficult to convey in a written brief , get put aside in the wake of some of the greater or more complex technical requirements. One could imagine a multimedia brief which would actually carry conditional signals, so that when the design is put through a test routine any conflict with the conditions would trigger a warning.'

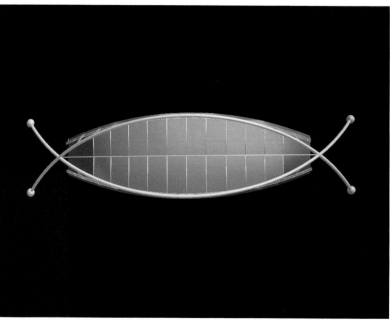

Two views of a competition project for a bridge

This is an extension of the way computer people work with information already. Instead of working within a prescribed program for a given task, the user opens a document and can then call up any or function or utility to handle the document. The document file can be a drawing, a text, a database, even a formula: it can move between programs in a fully compatible way. The advent of the C++ programming language and object-oriented software engineering has made this all the more possible; indeed data interchange has become crucial to some professions.

Within the world of architecture there is a movement to make changes that in a way

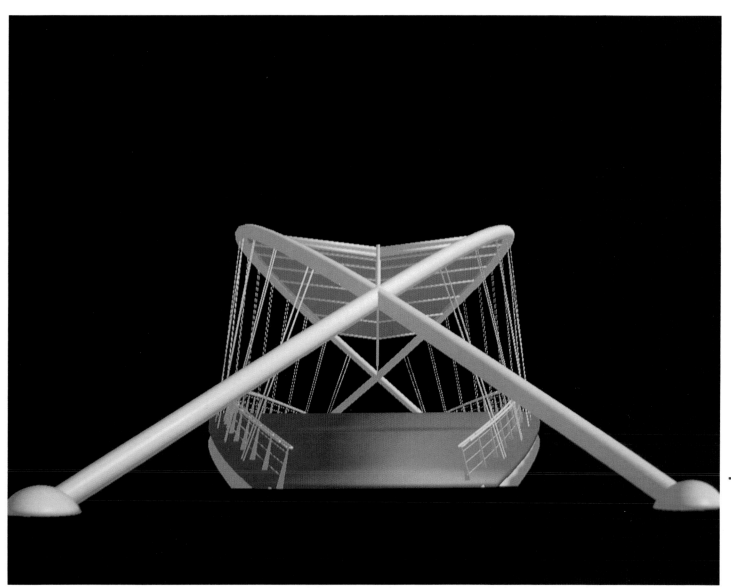

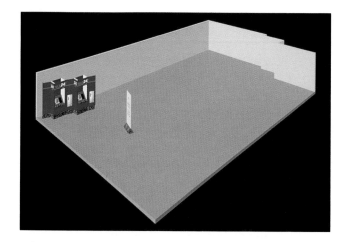
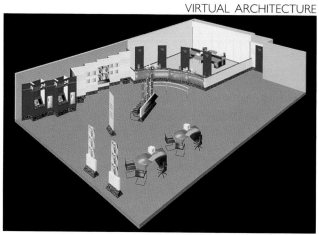

Assembling the interior fittings for a bank

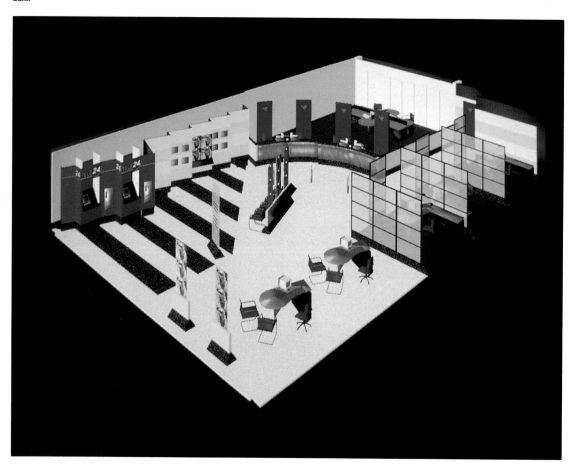

reflect the openness of the new systems. Architects are becoming specialists in the wide range of skills that are needed for the team required to complete a built environment, a team comprising civil and structural engineers, surveyors, services engineers, landscapists, HVAC experts, facilities managers and so on. These different disciplines need to interface with each other and so the right links between the groups in the team are critical, a mirror of the critical necessity for the different softwares used by different specialists to interface correctly. The architect is becoming the person who mediates the process, who controls the active model, to the extent that there is even some pressure on national professional bodies to recognize as architects some people who have not necessarily had the conventional experience of designing and building.

As to computer hardware, in the future what is possible now will become the norm. By this I mean that from the present computer screen and keyboard the latter will be the first to go, replaced by voice-activated systems of input. And the screen will disappear, to be replaced with a projector, probably based on fibre-optic technology, able to project on any chosen surface, or even all around one. The mouse will become a remote control device similar to the ones we now use for television sets and music systems. It is archaic in this day and age to be working with such mono-directional machinery as the conventional computer terminal.

Furthermore, in terms of its perceptual and frequency range, sight is one of humanity's least powerful senses. It is a delusion to think

Two interiors of the Lloyds building by Richard Rogers, visualized on Sonata

The entrance hall and interior of offices

for a telephone company

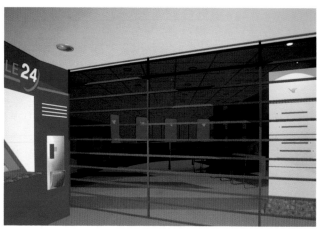

Four views of the fitting of interior offices
for a bank, and three views (*facing page*)
of a traditional housing development, all
rendered in Sonata

Two views of a competition project for
the Singapore Radio Tower

of the eye as all powerful. This delusion is becoming even clearer as we explore the macro and micro worlds around us, through nuclear physics and astronomy. Not only will our way of visualizing the world be increasingly influenced by this invisible knowledge, but the way we address virtual worlds will also be as much through our other senses as through sight. This may lead to new parameters for our physical environment, in helping to explore which the computer will be a thinking tool, not merely programmed to run fixed routines.

If we are going to get unhooked from our computers, no longer tied to the fixed screen nor to the predetermined tracks of a program, formatting this human-computer interface is going to become a crucial question. It will have to evolve radically, just as the future form of computers will perhaps be a bracelet and a purse, or a mike clipped to the collar. This machine will be not just a servant but an agent, to use Negroponte's term, able to execute specific commands and exercise a general judgement.

Visualization of a high-rise office building in Hong Kong

Two renderings of the Peak Project, a
new building overlooking Hong Kong by
Terry Farrell & Partners.

Alternative algorithms

The USA - and California especially - has been the source of most of the software used on today's computers. That position, created thanks to America's massive military and aerospace investment in the Cold War years, is now not being eroded as much as shared with programmers in Europe and elsewhere. It is alleged, for example, that a number of small 2D CAD programs were written in South Africa as sanctions-busters, some of them even financed by ArmsCorp, the apartheid government's weapons purchasing and manufacturing company. Graphisoft is a CAD program from the other end of the political spectrum. According to Gábor Kazár, vice-president of international business development, the initial software was designed by a group of mathematicians at the Technical University of Budapest during the communist period. They had devised a set of algorithms for modelling solids on screen (as opposed to earlier CAD programs which had begun life as two-dimensional drawing programs and grown up into three-dimensions).

In any other communist country, deprived by the Cold War of access to modern computer technology, these algorithms would have remained an interesting curiosity. But on the other side of the world a computer company, Apple, was looking for new applications for a new machine, the Macintosh. Hungary's open attitude to trade with the West made it possible for the team to finish the first version of ArchiCAD, and to negotiate help for a project which Apple might have otherwise considered insufficiently ready. There was common ground on the approach to the user, and Apple's business skill was to help Graphisoft develop the product in the market: the first Mac version

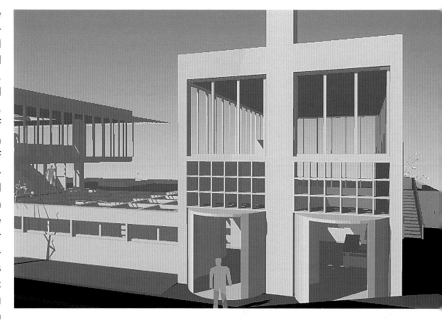

Images created using Graphisoft's ArchiCAD program

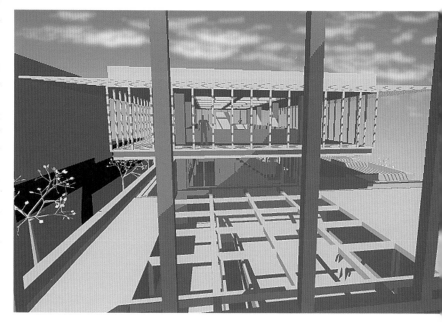

Torres de Campolide, Lisboa, 1993

João Paciência, arquitecto

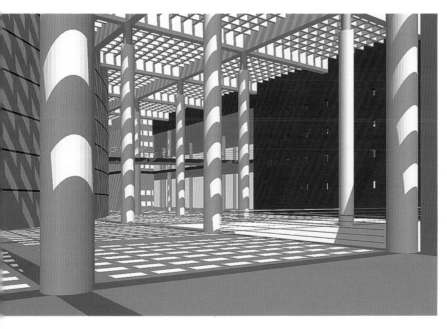

was launched in 1984, and a Windows version was released in 1993. Graphisoft has built up a customer base of over 16,000, mainly in the European market, and their approach to computing shows up interesting differences between the two hemispheres.

In the USA the tendency has been to create broad-based low-cost software, with add-on packages for specific tasks. The standard Autodesk program can handle 2D and 3D design of any kind, for example. An engineer can customize the main program by adding sub-routines for specific engineering tasks, an architect likewise. The current list of AutoCAD third party products runs to several hundred, covering a wide range of applications. (One other CAD software house even includes a program for undertakers to design coffins in its third-party applications list. The virtual funeral cannot be far off.) In Europe there has been much more of a tendency to develop specific stand-alone products for a single market group, such as architects or structural engineers. This approach, shared by Graphisoft, has been capable of creating a dedicated product, clearly mission-oriented.But such a program will, in terms of price, inevitably be in the central/high band of CAD products. It also demands excellent provider/user relations, dealer support and customer liaison, as well as generating a program that must meet all the end-user's requirements. After all, the investment made by the architect goes to the heart of the work to be done in an office.

Graphisoft's success in developing a world class CAD program from inauspicious beginnings, and the ways in which they have reached the market by providing an archi-

José Soalheiro, arquitecto

Associação de Industriais do Minho, 199

tecturally dedicated service, are in interesting contrast to other software histories. Their decision to follow a modelling based approach rather than a vectored graphic one does also set their programs apart from others, though they deliver the same quality results. Developing the program's capacities in the future will include facilities management units, as well as interface software for high-level rendering programs and for third party developer support.

More interestingly, the company are reflecting on how to make high-cost programs available to a specialist market in the future. Firstly there is the risk all software developers face of unlicensed copies and even piracy (though Graphisoft programs, like many other expensive dedicated programs do have an electronic lock which fits into an output slot, and without which the program will not run). With an inexpensive program, regularly purchasing updates is a reasonable expense, but with a more expensive program not only are costly upgrades resented by users, but also not all the facilities built into the upgraded program are of equal value to each user. In this context software ownership is not as important as software access and service. One of the options looked at, as an alternative to upgrade sales, is a downloadable system, whereby the user gets the whole program for a low price, but can unlock certain additional facilities as needed, on payment of an additional fixed fee, or fee for use. This allows the user to configure the system to the requirements of the job or the practice. An alternative approach, 'Pay Per Use', is to charge an annual fee for use (on a time or paper use basis). This would reduce the initial cost of a

**Images created using Graphisoft's
ArchiCAD program**

program by a factor to ten or twenty, and only involve payment for time actually on system. Such innovative approaches would allow the potential user to evaluate a new program before making what is a sizeable investment.

Just as there are competitors to Autodesk in the general CAD field (MiniCAD is widely used by architects who prefer Apple Macs to PCs) and competition for rendering programs (Electric Image and Ray Dream are two competitors with 3D Studio, for example), so there is a range of dedicated products available in Europe as well. Arkey, in the Netherlands, and Genesys in the UK have both concentrated on adding facilities management packages to specific architectural CAD packages. In Germany CAD BAU 400 is a parametric program that has been adopted by IBM as its preferred software for OS/2 users. Also in Germany speedikon has been developed by IEZ, formerly a research group at the Technical University in Darmstadt, and offers an intelligent building model through a linked database. Originally developed for use on Unix, Speedikon is now available with both Microstation and AutoCAD front ends, allowing the user to continue with a familiar command structure while accessing intelligent modelling features. This is intended to help IEZ reach new markets in the USA and the Pacific. Star Informatic, based in Belgium, also offers CAD packages in 2D and 3D aimed directly at the architecture and construction, cartography and surveying, and facilities management markets. Their core product, Star, also offers a relational database that updates information on the building as design elements are added or changed on the model. Star have been particularly successful in moving into the Japanese market, with their systems in use at a number of Japanese universities.

This proliferation of different but related programs, all designed with a high degree of interconnectivity, normally through the .dfx file format, and often working under Windows or with similar click-and-point graphical user interfaces with menu listings and dialogue boxes, offers the architect both opportunity and choice. Rather than trying to pick favourites, it would be better to ask what the architect's office of the future will expect in terms of CAD facilities.

For some commentators, the answer is obvious: there will be no more architects. The architectural profession is under terminal threat. In the UK, for example, the government was at one point recently seriously considering deregistering architects, allowing anyone, in effect, to offer architectural services. In France, on the other hand, the strict regulation of architects's fees and services, and the costly necessity of competitions for even small-scale public buildings, rather than creating equality of opportunity, are being seen as making the medium-sized practice almost unviable. In the USA, where regulation is not an issue, there are tensions between architects and interior designers, who are being increasingly called interior architects. A further threat is posed by the success of design and build contractors, who offer the property developer a complete service without any recourse to an outside architect. This doom-laden vision was excellently expressed in BBC television's Late

Three screen shots from MicroStation, a high-end specialized CAD package by Bentley Systems

Show's television programme *Architecture Armageddon,* written by Martin Pawley.

Pawley highlighted the competition from outside and within the profession that was even leading architects to work for zero fees, and the strain on the profession from the growing numbers of architectural students fighting for fewer jobs. The general denigration of modern architecture in the popular press and the preference for a backward vision of architecture and urbanism in influential circles, notably those around Prince Charles have, in combination with the recession of the early 1990s, made the architectural profession - in the UK, at least - feel increasingly insecure. But the argument over who controls the creative aspect of a project, and who runs the design process is relevant all over the globe. The old metaphor of master and servant between architect and client (a metaphor which cuts both ways with a strong architect and an indecisive client) is no longer appropriate, and a new relationship needs to evolve, particularly with the construction and service complexities of modern buildings. If the architect is to survive as an independent professional in an increasingly competitive environment, the practice of the profession is going to have to change. In particular, if the architect is to remain the team leader, the architect's office is going to need not only design capabilities, but organizational and communication ones as well.

In this process the computer will be an essential tool. Within the architectural office the computer and plotter is already taking much of the routine off the drawing board and into the memory. This reduces staff

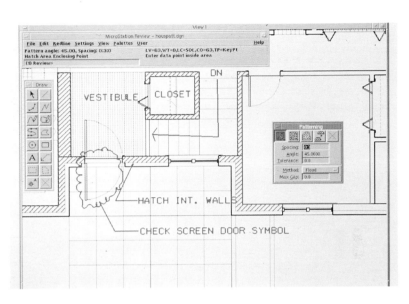

overhead costs, as well as freeing the architect's time for creative work. The fact that information on structural and decorative elements of all kinds, from steel beams and concrete mixes to lighting and sanitary fixtures, door furniture and ductwork, can be held on databases and imported directly into the model also saves time hunting up suppliers and estimates. It also allows the user of a parametric program to create the secondary information the client needs at the same time as the design. Properly handled, a parametric program, as we have seen, can create not only the master design, but the costings associated with it and a complete construction schedule.

Outside the office the ability of contemporary programs to create perspective drawings with a high degree of realism, as well as elevations and plans is extremely important in presenting the architect's ideas to clients and planning bodies. A recent change to French planning law obliges anyone submitting a proposal for any new building to include not only conventional plans and drawings, but also two rendered views of the final building, at least one of which must be from main street level. This *règlement environmentale et patrimoiniale* reflects the increasing public debate about the role of modern architecture in the urban fabric. Furthermore, the ability of programs such as MiniCAD and 3D Studio to generate video sequences and fly- or walk-throughs of proposed designs also enables the architect to explain a proposal more cogently than even a scale model can, as well as offering potential users the chance to evaluate a building before construction.

Three award-winning designs executed on Star Informatic systems by Images & Dimensions, Liège, (*above*), by students at the Kure National College of Technology (*facing, top*) and Roland Faessler of Orca in Switzerland

The new technology - not only the computer and the current high-level CAD programs but also information technology generally - will draw the architect from a position of relative independence even deeper into the process of creating buildings. For most architects this will be a welcome development, especially if in the process the architect regains or retains the high ground of control over the design and its evolution into a finished building. So the architect's office will not only feature electronic drawing and databases, but an electronic network sending out and receiving information from the other partners in the team, on the client's side and on the construction side, as well as generating high-quality static and moving images to present the project to planners and to the public. And this will lead, as David Clarke of Autodesk has pointed out, eventually to the adoption of Virtual Reality as a medium not only of communicating a design before construction, but even as a design tool in itself. To the uses architects are already making of available VR programs we will turn in the next chapter.

102

Images created in Electric Image: the Hyatt Hotel, Hong Kong, by Teresa Williams *(top)*, **the Jubilee Line Depot in London by Alan Davidson of Hayes Davidson and** *(facing) Bath House* **by Alan Arko of Electric Image**

Cyberspace simulated

Cyberspace, the Internet, information superhighways, virtual reality: modish phrases, more often used than understood. Cyberspace, as we have seen, is a term invented by writer William Gibson to describe total human-computer interaction, a world in which humans will interface directly with data, at a wholly convincing level of realism and with real world effects: a data protection system can kill a hacker. It is also used as a generic term for virtual communities that exist only through computer contact, such as the Lucasfilm Habitat project. The Internet is a network of computers linked by telephone lines and modems, in which anyone can participate. It grew out of the need for defence researchers spread across America to exchange computer data directly, then extended into an electronic mail service for academics, and now into the wider world, both geographically and socially. It is a wholly self-regulating system, with its own arcane jargon and informal rules of etiquette.

On the information superhighway the Internet approaches cyberspace It is a physical construct, envisioned as a network of fibre optic cables linking every building in the world, personal, public and commercial, and allowing for the transfer of not only phone messages and fax, but data, video, and interactive entertainment and business. As a concept the information superhighway suggests that there are commercial opportunities in the transfer of data between companies (just as major financial centres are linked by permanent data phone lines at present) and organizational savings for businesses and workers who will no longer be dependent on specific physical locations. Underlying all of

Head-mounted display (HMD) for use
with Virtual Reality

106

these concepts is the central notion that it is not atoms that are important, but bits, the messages not the media, as Nicholas Negroponte has so ably argued. Once an item can be put into digital form (whether it is a newspaper feature, your photo of a friend's wedding, a video of a classic film, the results of a survey on political attitudes, or whatever) then it can be transferred from one medium to another electronically. The information ceases to be dependent on its format. This process is happening all about us. The text for this book, for example, was written in one computer program, seen and checked on screen by one author, faxed to the other author in Hong Kong, put on a disc for the London publisher who sent it by electronic mail to the American publisher, then imported into a different program to be made up into pages, then passed to the printer who assembled it with scanned - that is, digitized - versions of the illustrations, then printed and bound. At different times, in terms of atoms, the text you are reading was a screen image, a piece of fax paper, an electronic message, a second and different screen image, a piece of film and the paper you are holding. But the bits remained the same.

Virtual Reality takes the idea of digitization to a further extreme. If anything can be digitized, then it would be possible to represent the world - or part of the world, or an imagined space - as a wholly digitized environment, with which humans, through a computer, could interact as freely as they do with real objects in the real world. This concept opens up a vast range of intellectual and practical possibilities, and every

A virtual interior, showing the user's
hand, created by ATMA, Milan

improvement in the technology creates more opportunities. To date VR has been applied to flight simulators, to military training for helicopters and tanks, to long distance surgery, and to teleconferencing. It is used in developmental engineering, in pharmaceutical research, in the nuclear industry, in entertainment, and in architecture and planning.

The basic requirements for VR programs are in two parts. The first is a system of tools to build the virtual world. The first building blocks can be files from existing CAD or rendering programs, and the computer 'engine' links these into a wholly interactive virtual space, so that the positional and functional relations between the different elements are established and the connections made. The second part is an operational system that allows the user - or users - to explore the virtual space and interact with it. Clearly, the degree of detail and 'accuracy' in the virtual world is a question both of programming skill and computer memory, and the success of the playback element a function of how rapidly the program can react to the user's change of position and view. The operational system must be able to accommodate, in the vision and information it presents, all the actions in the virtual space the user makes, in realistic perspective from a moving viewpoint, and in real time.

There are two basic forms of operational system: immersive and non-immersive. The image of the user armed with headset and directional mouse is familiar from fantasy games, which have been an important force in developing fully immersive technology. The data glove, and now the data suit, also

Interior details of a nuclear reactor, created by Division for Electricité de France

provide fuller contact with the virtual space. Non-immersive technologies include screens with trackballs (pressure-sensitive three-directional mice) , or stereo screens with special viewing glasses to give a three-dimensional effect. In both immersive and non-immersive VR, the key factor is the user's autonomy of movement within the virtual space. This is what distinguishes true VR from architectural flythroughs or other intermediate simulations where the user's path is not self-chosen but controlled by the program.

In architecture and design VR has been applied to assess aspects of a design before building work commences. For a client building a new warehouse, for example, a virtual warehouse can be built through which a fork lift truck can be driven, in real time, to check that turning circles and access points are correctly placed. In just such an exercise the engineers at Superscape discovered that in fact the truck would get stuck in certain corners. The client estimates that checking the design with VR saved about £200,000 ($300,000) on the redesign costs that would have been incurred had the problem been found once the building was up. In another case, a trade exhibition organiser used a virtual vision of a trade hall to place and design exhibitors' stands, giving their clients the chance to assess the stand designs fully on screen before construction started. Division have been working with fire department authorities to evaluate the placing of fire exits, and to visualize evacuation procedures for new buildings at the planning stage.

Another major project for Division was to recreate the interior of a nuclear reactor building for Electricité de France, the French

state-owned power company. EDF wanted to check the safest procedures for maintenance and refitting. By testing different paths through the interior assembly, and monitoring the radiation exposure and time of each, Division and EDF were able to come up with the best line of attack for each operating procedure which would reduce the radiation risk to the workers involved to a minimum. These tests were run both on an on-screen system and in immersive form, since the virtual world could be easily accessed in either manner.

One of the most ambitious immersive VR projects of recent date is the virtual house created by Division for Matsushita Electronic Industries in Japan, one of the world's most innovative electronic companies. The interior is that of a modern Japanese two-storey house, with living rooms, kitchen, bedrooms and bathrooms. Wearing a headset and holding a three-directional mouse you can explore each room, turning on and off the lights, running the water in the bathroom (with realistic sound effects), opening and closing curtains, doors and cabinets, moving furniture. A ghostly grey hand appears in the space before you, matching the position of the hand and mouse in real space, and allows you to reach out and turn on taps, open drawers and push door handles. The detailing is complete. There is a view out of the windows, reminiscent of a Sunday afternoon in middle England in November, however. Architecturally the house is at best undistinguished, and the blue-on-white flock wallpaper in the living room is definitely not something for the modernists. But the architecture was not Matsushita's main aim in creating the virtual house.

Two interiors of the Matsushita house, designed by Division

DIVISION

In part, Matsushita thought that creating a fully-working domestic interior was about the most challenging project they could come up with to prove to themselves the range and validity of virtual reality as an architectural tool. In fact modelling a pure white Corbusian space would have been a good deal easier. A number of commentators have suggested that VR will take a long time to appeal to architects, because the control of detail is far from sufficient. The Matsushita project shows how much progress can be made using top-level systems and equipment, in this case Division's dVS software running on a Silicon Graphics Onyx platform

The other explanation for the project is that part of Matsushita's main business is designing air conditioning and heating systems, for the domestic market as well as for industrial and commercial spaces. Another part is making domestic electronic products, mainly under the Panasonic label. The virtual house gives them a testbed to evaluate new designs, which can be imported into the display from CAD files without the expense and delay of making a series of full-scale models. Their engineers and designers can review how their products would look and could be operated in a typical setting. The program is set up to evaluate air and heat flows: a stream of green bubbles rises from the rice cooker, demonstrating how the steam moves from the pot to the ceiling fan. A virtual toolbox is there for the user: grasp an electric torch, and it projects a beam of light wherever it is pointed.

Airflow patterns rendered in the Matsushita house (*above & top*) **and the virtual toolkit** (*facing page*).

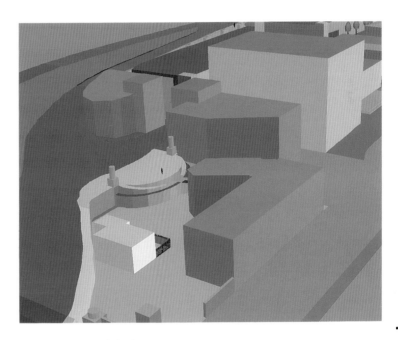

Preliminary massing study for the
Quayside project, created on Superscape

Views of the Newcastle Quayside created
by Real Time Design (*this and following
pages*)

Designing a single house for the immersive visitor is one challenge: creating a new cityscape on the screen is a rather greater one. Trevor Pemberton and his team at Real Time Design have, since 1991, been building on screen the new Quayside development in Newcastle-upon-Tyne, in the north-east of England. Newcastle was a major port on the east coast of England, particularly for the coastal coal trade down to London, and was a centre for shipbuilding and other heavy industries. With the decline of the coal trade, shipbuilding and industry, the quays and docks of Newcastle fell increasingly into disuse, and many have been derelict since the 1970s.

In 1987, the Tyne & Wear Development Corporation was given funds by the Department of the Environment to develop a new urban programme for Newcastle and the surrounding area. Starting with a number of small pilot schemes, in 1991 the Corporation's strategy changed, and one of their new flagship projects was the Quayside development. This is a twenty-five acre site on the banks of the river Tyne, following the contour of the river, downstream from the famous Tyne Bridge, itself a reduced scale study for the Sydney Harbour Bridge. The development plan will create 330,000 square feet of office space, together with retailing, hotel facilities, a pub and restaurants, carparks and over 200 private houses.

The site is long, narrow and sloping (the crossfall from the boundary road to the edge of the river is about fifty feet). There are two listed buildings on the site, a warehouse

building for the Co-operative Wholesale Society, listed Grade II, and a 17th century Sailor's Bethel or hospital (where Real Time Design now have their offices). A master plan for the whole development was produced by Terry Farrell & Partners, and accepted by the Corporation.

Their next problem was to develop the master plan in two ways: firstly to sort out the infrastructure problems implicit in developing an area abandoned for two decades, and secondly to attract private investment for the different elements on the site. Farrell's plan was an outline only, since the commissions for individual buildings were to be awarded independently. A conventional fixed model was therefore not appropriate. At that time Trevor Pemberton was acting as a consultant on Virtual Reality projects for a local high school, and he showed his work in visualizing cityscapes and factory floors to the Corporation. The result was an invitation to create a massing study in VR, to analyse the placing of the different elements and the infrastructure links. The success of this initiative led to a commission to develop a fully-detailed model.

The first stage was to scan the Farrell master plan onto a contoured map of the area, then place and map the various infrastructure elements, using the plans supplied by Ove Arup, the consulting engineers. The software used was Superscape, developed by UK-based Dimension Ltd, running on a Unix workstation. The plans and elevations were then converted into rendered three-dimensional images in perspective. Once this virtual world was constructed, adding new

buildings as they were designed by individual
architects and making changes to the overall
plan as requirements changed was both rapid
and straightforward.

Individual buildings are designed and rendered as separate files and then imported into
the main model. This, Trevor Pemberton explains, is simply because it is faster to do so,
and allows others to access the main file instead of locking it up while a building is being imported from CAD files. And removing a
building for changes to the design are faster
as well. Terry Farrell's design for the pub/res-
taurant uses a series of sails on the roof, re-
calling the sailing ships that used to throng
the port. There is also a deliberate, slightly
jokey echo of the Sydney Opera House, as
the pub is just downstream of the Tyne Bridge,
from which the final Sydney Bridge was devised. Other buildings on the site have been
designed by Hadfield Cawkwell Davidson and
Ryder Nicklin.

This adaptability is not the only reason for
choosing a virtual model. The different con-
stituencies the Development Corporation
needed to address were not all familiar with
reading architectural drawings and plans.
Though some physical models were commissioned for the project, a full model would be
costly and time-consuming to change. And a
model can only be used by a few people at
the same time, while inverted periscopes to
study access and perspectives at street level
are not always easy for non-specialists to use.
In the virtual environment, the user can stand
at street level and see the mass of surrounding buildings. This proved particularly valu-

**Two views of the Quayside project in
Newcastle-upon-Tyne, by Real Time
Design**

able in placing the utilitarian buildings such as multi-storey car parks. Changing their proportions in the virtual model allowed the architects, the Napper Collerton Partnership, to tuck the edges of the building into the side of the site, reducing its visual impact. This in turn left more of the car park budget available to design a high quality and more aesthetically pleasing front facade for the public face of the car park.

The virtual model is a lot more portable than a physical model, and so could be taken out to the community for consultation. According to Michael Baker, project director for Quayside, 'the Quayside in Newcastle is really an extension of the city . We needed to involve the community in what we planned to do, as well as being able to communicate effectively with designers, planners and potential building purchasers. Virtual Reality is a fantastic tool for this.' A monthly monitoring panel meeting is held with representatives of the local community, developers and city councillors. The VR system has been taken to a number of these meetings to provide an easy means of visualizing the site. For example, seeing their proposed building in three dimensions on the model allowed the Ouseburn Water Sports Centre to initiate a number of changes to make it more suitable for their needs, before even the foundations were laid. Such changes would have been too costly to make in the finished or partially finished building. There have been many valid and useful contributions to the development of the project from the public, and the virtual system has facilitated this process of communication.

Facade analysis for the Quayside project.

Trevor Pemberton is also recording a number of fly- and walk-through videos of the site as a whole and of particular locations. These are valuable marketing tools for presenting the project to potential purchasers and tenants. In 1993 Newcastle hosted the Tall Ships Race, and are now in discussion with the organizers to see if they can again be hosts of this famous event in the year 2001. Using the virtual model, the city can show the race organizers how the Quayside will look in that year from any perspective. 'That is a unique - and very persuasive argument,' as Michael Baker points out.

Assembling the first massing model took Real Time Design about six months, and adding individual buildings as the designs become available is a matter of days. Given that the timescale for the whole development is a decade, the time spent in investing in the virtual model is definitely worthwhile, and makes a strong case for using similar models for development projects on this scale in the future. The value of VR as a development, consultation, marketing and presentation technique is clear from these examples. As VR technology becomes more accessible (programmes such as Superscape VRT already run on a Pentium PC platform), more architects will be able to put it to use, not just on actual projects, but as a design tool for modelling virtual worlds.

In April 1995 an event occurred which suggests that building in VR is moving closer to the everyday. The Mayor of Barcelona and the Spanish Minister for Industry cut the ceremonial ribbon to mark the opening of a brand new building project, the Barcelona

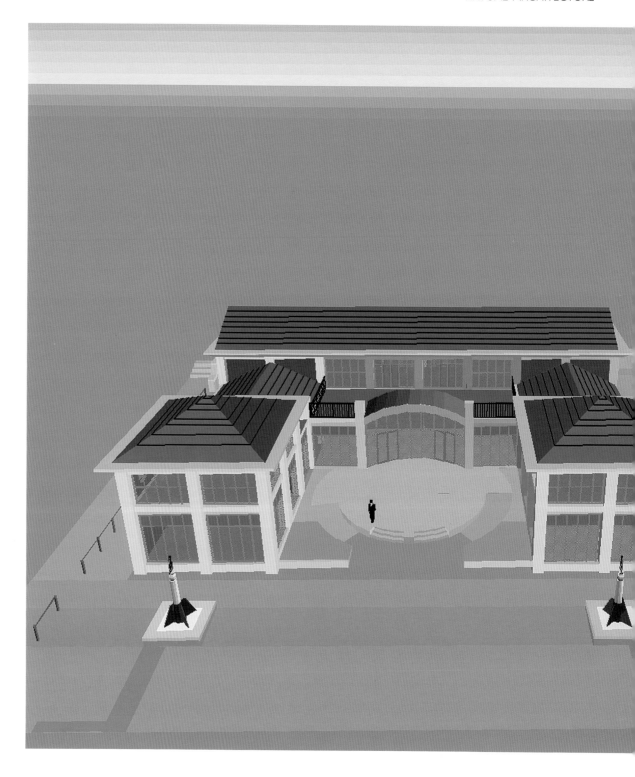

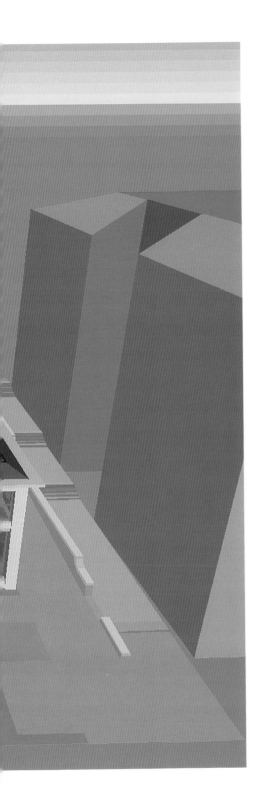

Technology Forum. Cutting ribbons is part of a mayor's regular routine. But in this case the ribbon was a virtual one, cut using a pair of VR scissors by the mayor and the minister wearing VR headsets.

Sited in the north of the city of Barcelona, the new Technology Forum covers some 11,000 square metres. It is built principally of concrete and steel and designed as three separate transverse concourses with two internal patio areas; as pavilions in Barcelona go, it is architecturally correct rather than astonishing. The reasons why so many turned out for the opening were twofold: firstly, this was the first example in Spain of a building being opened using the technology of virtual reality. The Technology Forum had been visualized (in just three weeks) by Barcelona-based VR specialists, RTZ, using Superscape VRT virtual reality software. For the opening ceremony, hosted by a 'virtual actor' called Nestor, the mayor and the minister donned VR headsets and were able to explore the new virtual-reality created Technology Forum (running on a network of Pentium PCs) and meet each other - virtually. The ceremony culminated with the cutting of a virtual ribbon using a pair of VR scissors.

The second reason for the enthusiasm of the audience lies in the function of the Technology Forum itself. The project was started in 1991 after the Olympics with the objective of bringing a centre of technological excellence and learning to a very depressed and poor area of the city of Barcelona. Money for the development of the Forum was raised by a grant from the EU (under the auspices of the STRIDE programme), investment from the City of Barcelona and from an organization known as Barcelona Activa. The Technology Forum will provide a business centre for small high technology companies working in such areas as virtual reality, multimedia and telecommunications, an exhibition centre (Expo Forum) and extensive workshops and classrooms, offering different types of training in new technology for the young, the unemployed, as well as to business people wishing to gain a better understanding of specific techniques.

For the people of Barcelona, virtual reality is literally part of the foundations of the Technology Forum. The initial designs for the building were visualized, again using Superscape VRT, by RTZ more than a year ago, and the disc carrying the 'virtual world' was buried under the foundation stone of the new Forum. For the mayor, it was in a sense his second tour of the building, as the original virtual design had been seen by him when the competition to build the centre was staged. His return visit, in HMD, is a vindication of the value of VR systems in making design concepts accessible to the widest possible public.

Three virtual views of the inauguration of the Barcelona Technology Centre, 1995, created by RTZ in Superscape

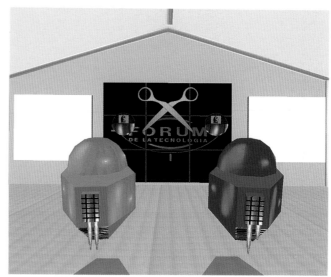

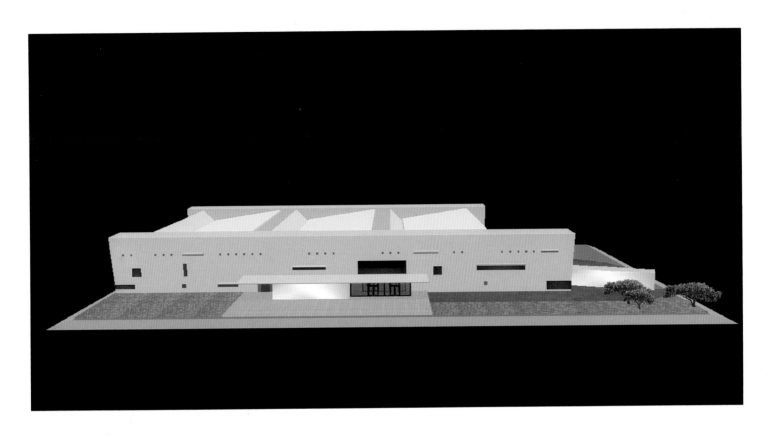

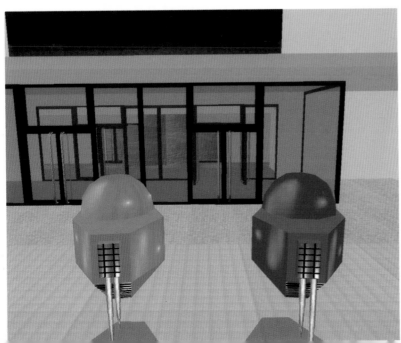

Moving into the light

Moving into the light

The problem of developing lighting designs for the interiors and increasingly the exteriors of buildings fall into two categories. One is the technical question of ensuring that the lighting level is adequate for the work to be done in the building. The second is the visual one of showing the lighting effect on a drawing (on-screen or on paper) in a way that will allow architect, client and planner to evaluate the intended appearance.

The technical subject is often covered by regulations, specifying required levels of light in different settings. Often such regulations are mandatory in buildings to which the general public have access. They set levels of light either to be achieved at eye level, or more generally, on the working plane - the standard height of a desk. These levels are calculated in lux, a measurement of the amount of light in lumens falling on a square metre surface. (In the United States of America, the calculations are made in foot-candle, being the illumination in candle-power to the square foot, so that one lux is roughly ten foot-candles.) For a cinema auditorium, the level may be 100 lux (1000 foot candles): in an office 400 lux (4000 foot-candles): in the operating theatre of a hospital it would be 700 lux (7000 foot-candles). Different light sources give out different amounts of light: a conventional 100 watt tungsten lamp creates about 1200 lumens, a 150 centimetre 65 watt fluorescent tube about 5000 lumens. The level of light at a particular point in a space is therefore a combination of the distances from the point to the various light fittings, and the light levels emitted by them. To this must be added the effect of any reflectors or diffusers in the

Lighting effects on the frontage of a gentlemen's club in Tokyo, created by Giuliano Zampi in Sonata

actual fitting, and the reflectance of the surfaces in the space. Different colours and different textures absorb more or reflect more light, and this will contribute to the overall lighting level and quality.

Lighting manufacturers supply the technical information on the output of their lamps and their fittings to users, often in the form of polar curve charts, which show the intensity and spread of light at different distances from the source. Specialist lighting designers are on hand to advise on lighting schemes for particular spaces, and often form part of the team for large projects. Calculating the light levels at different points in a space can be done using a computer program. The most recent of these is a Windows-based program distributed by SLI International in Geneva, in which the user can specify the shape of the space to be lit, input the fittings and lamps to be used and their positions in the space, and the program then calculates the level of light, in lux, at various levels (normally on the ceiling, on the floor and on the work plane). This program has been designed by Axel Stockmar and his colleagues in Germany, who have been active in setting European standards for measuring the light emission of lamps, so allowing the user to include not only SLI's Sylvania lamps but other manufacturers' products in their calculations. The program and its ancillaries are straightforward in use provided that one has a grasp of the basic principles of lighting.

Two views of the glazed facade of a building, rendered by Giuliano Zampi, showing the effects of different lamp colours

The success of any lighting calculation program depends not merely on its accuracy in calculating luminance and distances, but also on the level of calculation. Take an imaginary light beam from a point source in the middle of a cubic space. The light leaves the lamp in all directions, then is reflected by the walls, floor and ceiling. This reflected light is re-reflected off the opposite surface, then re-re-reflected and so on, almost infinitely. Each time the light is reflected, some of its energy, and so its lux value, is absorbed by the surface it hits. Calculating this to the ultimate degree is impractical, not to say impossible. So most programs set in advance the level of iterations, that is to say the number of repeat calculations the program makes before fixing the

result. Whether the user prefers a program with a high level of iterations (which will normally use more memory space and work slightly more slowly) or a simpler one, is probably best decided on the basis of the requirements of the job in hand. As a matter of practice, where lighting levels are critical, it is the architect's responsibility to ensure that the regulations in force are met by the proposed lighting design.

The question of creating 'realistic' light effects in computer images, rather than simply analysing the distribution of light, is a problem of a very different order. The rendered surfaces in solid modelled graphics are in fact sets of polygons with the same description, or repeated descriptions to create a pattern, for example for brickwork or planking. The number of pixels (the picture cells that make up the dots on a computer screen) in each polygon defined the degree of detail possible. Clearly, the more pixels per polygon, the more detail could be rendered. But the higher the number of pixels or polygons for a given screen area, the slower the computer could compute and render the image, and the more memory that would be required to store it. The jagged edges seen on some solid modelled images reflect this necessary compromise between clarity and speed. To create an effect of three-dimensionality, the computer used algorithms to decide which polygons were in front on which from a particular viewpoint, and removing the hidden ones from view. If the viewpoint changed, the hidden surface removal routine was recalculated from the new standpoint. As computers got faster chips and more memory, images could be

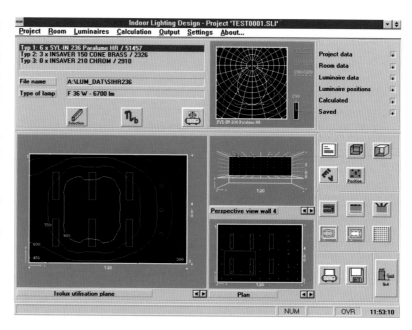

The main screen in the SLI/INL Lighting program

created using greater detail, and redrawing rates were faster. The polygon system created a working method whereby light effects could be reproduced. A further refinement of this approach was to use the process of recursive subdivision to create surface patches that could be as small as a single pixel. This smooths the surface down to the smallest unit on screen. It was devised by Ed Catmull while he was at the University of Utah: his company Pixar has also developed techniques to portray transparency through the technique he calls 'alpha blending' and on routines to texture-map two-dimensional images onto three-dimensional surfaces accurately.

The reiteration process described for lighting distribution programs uses Lambert's law, a principle discovered in the sixteenth century, and given practical application by artists ever since. Lambert pointed out that the quantity of light reflected from a surface depended on the angle at which the light struck the surface: perpendicular light would be wholly reflected, parallel light would not be reflected at all. Between the two, the proportion reflected would vary according to the cosine of the angle of incidence. It is this fact that enables us to perceive the shapes of objects. Imagine a three-dimensional object such as a sphere. If all the light were reflected back from its surface to us at the same intensity, it would appear to be a flat circle. The variation in light reflected across the change in shape of an object is what makes it visible.

Thus a cosine function can be applied to shade the appearance of an object according to its

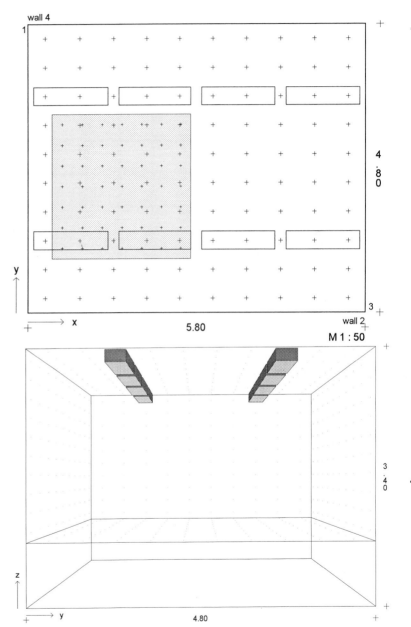

Plan and elevation of an interior created in the SLI/INL program

surface profile progressively, varying the value according to the change in surface angles from a fixed light direction. Parts of the object at a more oblique angle to the light would be darker. This procedure creates the appearance of objects bathed in a uniform, ambient light. Such a system was devised by Henry Gouraud for computer-generated images, and is called Gouraud shading. A further refinement of the procedure, called Phong shading after its inventor Bui-Tuong Phong, uses a greater degree of calculation, in effect smoothing out the surface structure before applying the calculations, and so increasing the graduations of light effect and so the degree of realism.

Lambert's law is the statement of an ideal: it applies to a perfectly diffusing surface, which will scatter diffuse light equally in all directions, or reflect directional light directly. We know from experience that in the real world surfaces are not perfect matte diffusers: they scatter some of the light falling on them and also reflect some directly. This is why we perceive highlights even on indifferently lit surfaces, and indeed such bright points are important visual clues in our reading of what we perceive. The proportion depends on the textures of the various surface material, as well as on the lighting conditions, but the general principle of a mixture between scatter and reflection can be used to create highlight effects in a computer-generated images, usually as part of a Phong shading process. This can be particularly useful in creating an image lit from several specific points, rather than in a general direction. A frequent architectural convention is to assume that the main light is coming from a point over the viewer's left shoulder at 40

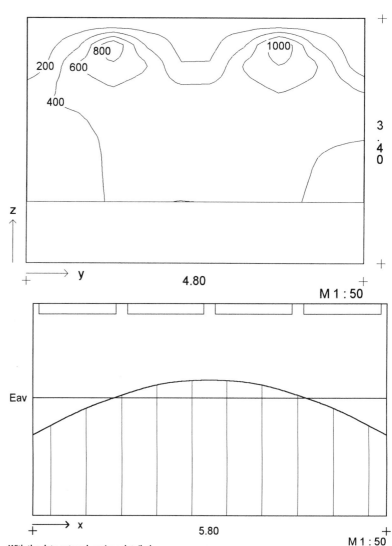

With the data entered, various detailed reports can be created on the SLI/INL program: isolux and illuminance distribution diagrams on a section (*top and above*), and lighting levels on the utilization plane and as a 3D graph *facing*).

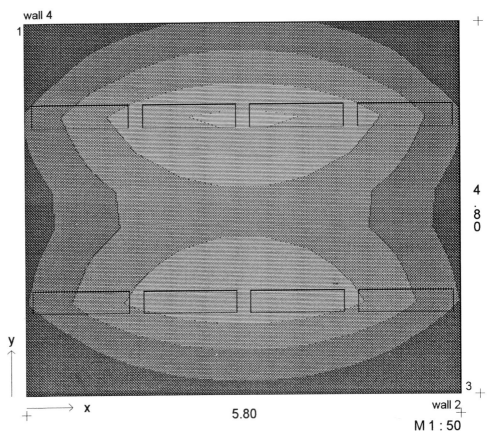

wall 4

1

wall 4

4
.
8
0

y

x

5.80

3

wall 2

M 1 : 50

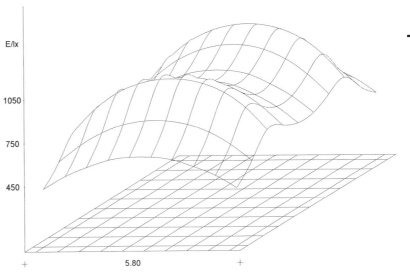

E/lx

1050

750

450

5.80

degrees vertically and horizontally to the line of sight.

The convention of line of sight is also used in a further technique for rendering computer images more realistically, called ray tracing. In this technique, devised by Turner Whitted, all the lines of light visible from the viewer's position are calculated and valued, including light rays passing between objects within a given scene. Thus the reflections in a mirrored surface would be calculated by the program, rather than drawn by the creator of the image. The technique is similar to the artist's device of placing a screen between artist and subject, and tracing out on the screen the image exactly as it appears. This is a lot easier to achieve in real life, and in computing terms requires superb programming, extensive memory and very fast computing times. The resulting images are highly realistic.

The step beyond ray tracing is radiosity, a system developed by Don Greenberg and his team at Cornell University. Radiosity performs the same kind of calculations as ray tracing, but without imposing a fixed position for the viewer. All the internal light paths within a given scene are calculated, at many layers of iteration, to create a virtually realistic pattern of light and shade, highlight and reflection. In effect the image of the computer is considered as being a closed system, and the elements within it divided into discrete patches (according to surface angle, curvature, colour, texture and so on). The interrelation of light between each pair of patches is then calculated. This is of course astonishingly complex (and if

The exterior of the Peninsula Hotel, Hong Kong, rendered by Giuliano Zampi in Sonata

part of the image is changed or moved the whole calculation has to be rerun.) To date, therefore, radiosity programs are only available on Unix workstations, though a PC version from ATMA in Milan will, it is claimed, be on the market by the end of 1995.

The advantage of radiosity over ray tracing, in terms of realism, is that it allows for even more precise calculations of exact lighting effects (though at the cost of more computer power and memory), especially for the subtle effects of diffuse light such as shadows and transparent colours. Its value in user terms lies in the absence of an initial viewpoint. If the viewer's position in a ray-traced image changes, the whole image needs to be redrawn from the new coordinates. But an image created under radiosity is independent, and does not have to be redrawn. As Enrico Checchi of ATMA explains 'for an animation the radiosity image has clear advantages in terms of speed, since the rate of motion across a ray-traced image depends on the computer's speed in redrawing the image from changing viewpoints. Where the animation is on a fixed path, for example on a planned architectural fly-through, this problem can be overcome by storing the individual frames and rerunning them as a computer video sequence. But in virtual reality environments, where the direction of movement in all dimensions is decided on by the viewer at whim, radiosity has a clear advantage. The only way, at present, in which ray tracing can compete is by coarsening the image definition, to save redrawing time. But this runs counter to the whole idea of using a rendering technique to increase realism.

Four interiors by ATMA, Milan, showing
the use of radiosity to render light
effects (*these pages & overleaf*)

For the architect, however, the question of rendering light effects accurately is not merely one of achieving some *n*th degree of realism on screen or on a printed version of the design. In the first place the architect's concern is not only with the image, but goes through and beyond it to the final building. So the on-screen image needs not only to have its own realism, but to be related with some exactitude to the lighting specification, in terms of lamps and fittings, that is proposed for the project in hand. At present even the most sophisticated radiosity programs cannot be input with specific lamp and fixture details. The angle and intensity of a light source can be entered, and the general tint of the light. But this data does not yet approach the detail and complexity of lighting information contained in calculation programs, nor does it allow for the subtle differences in actual and perceived light colour between different types of lamp.

One of the ground rules of discussing contemporary computer and software design is 'never say never'. So it is quite possible to speculate that radiosity programs could be extended to accept more precise lamp and fixture data. Alternatively, radiosity functions could be added to parametric programs to extend the image power of the program along with its database and interrelationality: the way in which Giuliano Zampi has been able to achieve extremely convincing lighting effects in Sonata is an example of this. But in terms of on-screen imagery such further refinements may not be justified, on economic or on practical grounds. For in fact

a screen is itself an illuminated image: pushing the screen to higher and higher levels of realism within the unreal confines of a rectangle of glass is an argument that at its core lacks logical sense. But the challenge of creating the realistic virtual image (and we will look at the logical contradictions of such a notion in the last chapter of this book) in a virtual reality is one that not only flight trainers and games designers but architects too are going to have face in the near future.

The Virtual Architect

The Virtual Architect

At Christmas 1994, the best selling computer game on the market was SIMCity 2000. In the game the player is the mayor of a new city, responsible for laying out roads and railways, water and power lines, for zoning land for residential, commercial and industrial use. A basic budget is available to meet these costs, and a variety of starting dates, from 1900 to 2050. Once the basic groundplan has been configured, the program takes over, populating the new town with simulated citizens (or Sims), who in turn build houses, shops and hotels, factories and churches. As the town develops, the Sims call for new facilities, schools, hospitals, police stations and parks. The mayor's job is to keep the town developing, controlling taxes and making new investments to maintain the quality of life for these invisible constituents. If the mayor fails, the Sims vote with their feet, and activity levels, population and so revenues, drop.

The game's appeal may lie in the fact that the player 'plays God' - to the extent that a space monster that eats buildings can also be released onto the hapless Sims. It also lies in the fact that living in a city is a problem many of us face daily - how many dinner party conversations come round to 'if I was running this town?' The game is well-structured, so that both a beginner and someone with some knowledge of planning can enter the game at their own level and enjoy it. The algorithms underlying the program show considerable subtlety and so finding the right balancing line between overspending and underinvesting is a real challenge. Typical players are said to range from schoolchildren to professional developers and academics, and sample cities, advice and commentary are widespread on the

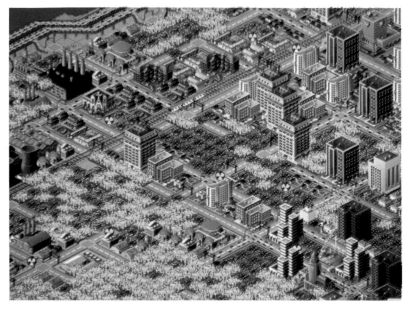

(*Above & facing*) **three screen shots from Sim City**

144

Internet, both through Maxis's own bulletin
board and on Compuserve under 'games',
where visitors find help from fellow-players.

The game poses a number of interesting questions for architects and planners: on the architectural side the fact that the Sims design their
own buildings is sometimes more than a dis-
appointment. There is one neo-adobe hotel,
for example, that has me reaching for the bull-
dozer button every time it appears. And if a
factory building becomes abandoned, the resulting image looks suspiciously Louis Sullivan.
The mayor's personal arsenal of buildings,
apart from a most grandiose town hall and also
a colonial governoresque mayoral residence,
does, however, include a choice of arcologies,
provided the game is played into the twenty-
first century.

From a planning point of view, the fact that
financial considerations are the main factors
for success in the game inhibits, for example,
investing in welfare programmes. High but affordable taxes are what keeps a city growing,
and growth is the key. The idea of a stable city,
balancing affluence and environmental impact,
seems foreign to the way SIMCity works - but
that may also be true of many real cities as
well! If the present game seems dominated by
the Reaganomic thinking of the 1980s, it is
worth pointing out that its creators, Fred
Haslam and Will Wright, are said to be working even now on a SIMWorld game, that will
use environmental and ecological factors. And
the game is an interesting challenge, particularly when the players choose to map the ter-
rain in their own way: imagine a version of
Paris with a straight river Seine, for example,
or New York without Central Park.

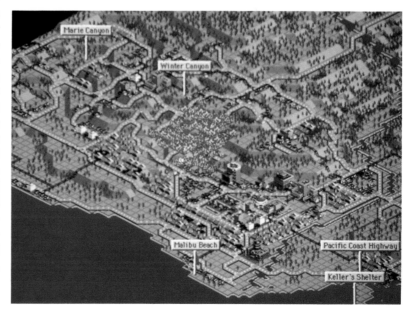

The success of SIMCity also tells us something about general perceptions of architecture and planning. Firstly and obviously, that it is a subject people relate to: if it wasn't fun being the mayor, few would play the game. More interestingly, people understand quite rapidly the notions of infrastructure, zoning and continuous development that are implicit in the structure of the game. And understanding the imagery on screen is also obviously not a difficult task, even though the continuous aerial perspective is not a familiar one, and even though the relative proportions of the buildings is not always to scale. In this respect SIMCity throws an interesting sidelight on how a wider public reads architectural imagery.

SIMCity, even more than most computer games, is about simulation. This is a subject of key importance in a world where we are increasing offered images that demand sophisticated evaluation if we are to read correctly their relationship with reality, indeed a world where the whole concept of reality is under stress, not only in computing and design, but in television and advertising, in contemporary science and contemporary philosophy. Benjamin Woolley's excellent book *Virtual Worlds* sets out two different definitions of virtuality in respect to contemporary computer simulations. He describes in detail how the idea of totally immersive virtual reality has developed from a number of different strands, starting in the American defence industry, through Ivan Sutherland's work with three dimensional views from helmets to the work of Autodesk and such pioneers as Ted Nelson, J Jay Lanier and even Timothy Leary. The work done at MIT's ArchMach (later the Media Lab) by Nicholas Negroponte and his team is also

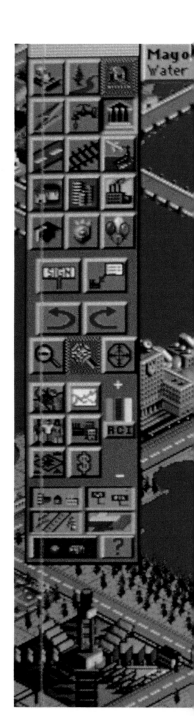

Arcologies for all: SimCITY's final solution to the housing problem

146

important here. The outcome of this approach, which is based on the premise that it is possible to create a physically and visually convincing world entirely within a computer-generated system of images, finds its apogee today on the one hand in top level flight simulation systems, and on the other in interactive games such as those produced by the company Virtuality in the UK. The term virtuality in this tauter definition means the creation of artificial worlds in a computer controlled environment.

Woolley's other argument, however, is that the process of scientific discovery, and developments in philosophy, particularly in linguistics, and in technology, particularly though not exclusively in computing, have forced upon the closing years of the twentieth century a redefinition of the whole idea of reality. In what ways can we talk about the real world, when to some extent we actually live in a virtual world, one in which the constraints imposed by social and political rules, by work systems, by personal and interpersonal behaviour are increasingly defined not in terms of physical absolutes but in terms of options that are mediated by cultural phenomena? At the same time, our understanding of the physical world is now moving to extremes of time and scale which defy any traditional notions of realism: medicine is unravelling the human gene, nuclear physicists search through sub-atomic particles for the elusive Higgs boson, astronomers argue each nanosecond of the Big Bang. Such worlds are virtual, in the sense that any visualization of them has to be metaphorical rather than real, though based on 'observed' scientific data.

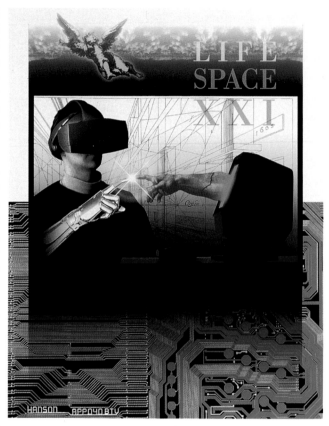

The cyberspace future, an image created by designers at Gensler Associates in California

148

The intellectual origins of this development can be traced to what has been called the Einstein revolution, even if Einstein himself, with his famous answer that 'God does not play dice', showed his disagreement with later developments such as Heisenberg's uncertainty principle, and the more recent proposals of catastrophe, chaos and crisis theory. Indeed these terms in themselves are perhaps sufficient to show to what extent late 20th century society is itself aware of losing its control over the world around it. As Woolley points out neither the term catastrophe or chaos, or indeed perhaps crisis is an accurate rendition of the main thrust of each of the theories in question since each of them, in slightly different ways, suggests that what appears to be catastrophe, chaos and crisis can be actually conceived as an ordered process, even if its rules of order are by no means immediately apparent. Virtuality in this sense represents the insecurity of the modern condition, our sense that we are living in a world whose true order is not only other than appearance, but possibly unknowable as well.

The combination of these two definitions of virtuality is best seen at work in the concept of cyberspace. This idea, as we have seen, was first expressed in the novels of William Gibson: *Neuromancer*, *Count Zero* and *Mona Lisa Overdrive*. Gibson predicts a future world in which computer technology will have advanced to the point where humans can interact directly with computer data, in a wholly 'real environment'. Gibson called cyberspace 'a graphic representation of data abstracted from the banks of every computer in the human system. Unthinkable complexity. Lines of light ranged in the nonspace of the mind, clusters and constellations of data. Like city lights, receding.' Cyberspace is a concept that has passed into computing language, and academic conferences and commercial R&D budgets are equally dedicated to defining and creating it. This may seem strange, rather like NASA technicians nipping to their copies of H.G. Wells and Jules Verne every time a problem with the moon lander came up. But given the long history of military developments in computing - one of the first virtual reality projects was a strategic nuclear warfare command and control system using virtual talking heads - the idea of pillaging fiction for ideas is not too surprising. One of the strengths of the development of computing has been the range of skills and visions brought to the new science (or new art, depending on your view) from many different disciplines and backgrounds.

In *Count Zero,* the second book in Gibson's trilogy, a passenger in a robot-driven hovercraft asks what make it is. A Rolls-Royce, the owner replies: 'they built a good car in the old days, the Arabs did.' Gibson's world is populated by wild hackers, bionic killers and elective mutants, deprived of history by

Rendering of the MGM lot, by Gensler Associates

war and of independence by the stranglehold of ruthless mega-corporations. The subtleties and elegance of Gibson's language (neural software implants are called, of course, microsofts), to say nothing of the dark ironies that flash through the text, have not been absorbed by all that have taken up his ideas. Cyberspace has spawned serious academic conferences, and in the popular press is the unleaded fuel for cruising the infobahn. But on the computing side, the notion of cyberspace is a dramatic extrapolation from the idealistic thinking of its time, such as the work of ArchMac, the Media Lab, and Ted Nelson's Xanadu project, among others.

In this brave new world of virtual uncertainty, the computer has played the central role. The development of computing systems has led to the theory of creating a virtual world, and the availability of computing techniques has enabled mathematicians, physicists and other scientists to look at problems, where previously there simply was no means of handling them. We have tried in the preceding pages to look at how contemporary computer systems, including virtual reality, are being put to work in architects' offices, and what the development of these new technologies has meant for architects. What will it mean in the future?

The second guiding principle, after 'never say never' is 'never say when'. The rate of change in the computing industry, and the direction of change, is wholly unpredictable. Take the example of computer platforms. Two or three years ago the idea that Apple Macs and PC's would become directly compatible was hardly thought possible. A year ago (this is written in May 1995) the Power Mac was released, which can transcribe directly files written in Windows and DOS applications, and this year a card is available for the standard Apple Mac which allows DOS and Windows software to be run on the Mac. (This meeting between major rivals is not merely the result of competitive pressure. It is part of a wider acceptance that communicability and compatibility lie at the heart of the future of computing for all users, as we have seen with open-endedness in CAD systems.) We live in interesting times, as the old Chinese curse puts it! So just when the architect will be able to move into the virtual office is an open question.

Office interiors by Giuliano Zampi

What the virtual architect may find there is, on the other hand, becoming clearer. In this book we have argued for the convergence of virtual reality, parametric database systems, and open access. At the start of our work this was a desirable and important ideal: along the way we have met many people who share that view, and, furthermore, who are busy trying to turn it into a reality. This notion of convergence has three main strands. Firstly it posits that virtual reality tools will enable designed spaces to be accessed as easily and as fully as real spaces. Secondly it demands that the information contained in such a model go beyond the simply visible aspects to embody a complete information set about the elements in the model and their interre lations. Thirdly it assumes that such a model can be created from any starting point and that data from any source can be incorporated into it.

So conventional wisdom envisages the architect opening the virtual door of the virtual building to the (hopefully real) clients, and taking them on a guided tour of the new premises. They step onto a virtual elevator, and it carries them effortlessly up, their presence animating advertising panels on the wall into life to explain the feelgood factors of Pepsi-Coke (in a virtual world other convergences are possible, after all.) From the roof a virtual helicopter flies them around the building - for those who do not prefer to fly around on their own.

But the conventional wisdom stops short of real understanding. In the virtual building the architect is Superman - or rather, more accurately and more politically correctly - Superchild. Like a child at play with a pile of building bricks, the virtual architect does not merely place a beam in the building, but moves it, bends and twists it at will. Rather than pushing open a virtual door, the architect can reach a virtual hand into a portfolio of window designs and pull out whichever alternative door fancy dictates. Rather than opening a window, the whole frame can be moved across the wall, the exterior view changing to match. At the same time, over the head phones, the architect will have a guide, a synthesized voice-projection of the building itself, saying what changes have been made to the air conditioning as a result of the move, to the costings, or whether the change improves the *feng shui* of the room.

Thus the virtual building is not the end product of the design process, but itself a starting point. You can start with a room ten foot square and push the walls around until you have the Alhambra or the first settlement on Tau Ceti. The possibilities are literally endless: you can create Cupid's palace from the Claude painting and bring Psyche into it.

This is, of course, what architects have always done - not only brought Psyche into the palace of Cupid, but created *ab initio*, from nothing. Every architectural design has started on a blank piece of paper, with a scribble, whether of words or lines. Paxton's design for the Crystal Palace, the building that validated glass and iron architecture in 1850, 145 years ago, began as a sketch on a telegraph form. Oscar Niemeyer's designs for the capital city of Brasilia, if legend is to be believed, covered a couple of sheets of foolscap. We tend to think of such gestures as heroic architecture, but they are also architecture at its most basic.

So what does the new technology add? The answer is that it offers both opportunities and risks. The opportunities are that these new tools will allow the architect not merely to create a personal vision, but to express that vision as fully as possible before it is built, or even if it cannot be built. And the vision can be shared on their terms, by non-architects. They can put on the headset or look into the screen, and experience the building, or the new town or the new office. The new technology gives architecture back to the world without taking it out of the hands of architects. It

also extends the domain of architecture in other important ways because the model will not only create a vision of the building, but through its related databases it will contain many of the other models of the building that other specialists need. This process will put the architect back into the centre of the team creating a building. That will put back into buildings the qualities of architecture.

The risks of the new technology run parallel with the opportunities. Negroponte has written convincingly that the human-computer interface should not be seen as being one of master and servant but rather of person and agent. John Walker broached the same idea when he talked about the wrong notion of building computers that were power saws when users wanted carpenters. In other words, the computer would not merely carry out tasks under supervision, but have some freedom of action, based on evaluating past choices by the user. The intelligent computer model of a building involves seeing the computer as agent, able, within parameters, to act independently. With an intelligent carpenter to hand, anyone can build a table: with an intelligent building machine, perhaps anyone can be an architect. In bringing the debate about architecture into the centre of the virtual building, architects will still have to remind their audience that the heart of architecture lies elsewhere.

The second risk of a technology that presents a 'realistic' view of architecture is that architecture becomes seen in parallel with other 're-alistic' views of the world such as television. A common platform - the screen - risks the category error of assuming that the media are the same. Media such as television, radio and film, and even books and magazines, have a single-event lifespan. They are matters of the day: they are tied ineluctably to their original present.

Often the ideas and images these media create have a wider and longer relevance - we all have in our heads a personal library of memorable images or words drawn from the plethora of the everyday. But in the true sense these images are metaphors only. They are detached from their basis of sense, which is in the actuality of their first transmission. As metaphors they may have immense power and influence on us, but they are essentially ephemeral.

Architecture is not ephemeral, and for architectural imagery to be confused with media imagery does architecture no good. This does not mean that a Chinese wall has to be erected between architecture and the media. The media are part of contemporary culture, as is architecture. One possibility that new technology offers is the building with a virtual surface, a moving kaleidoscope of images projected electronically onto a glass wall or through LEDs in the wall surface. Jean Nouvel's Mediapark project in Cologne uses the exterior walls as screens in this way. 'The volume and density of images and information compressed into the modern city,' he argues, 'renders the traditional formal definition of the exterior of a building absurd. Even practical signage is a source of information on the functional essentials of a building, but, like all imagery it has a poetic and dynamic role, part of the complexities of the whole. At the Mediapark the programme of images is part of the life of the building. Even the occupants

Jean Nouvel's Tour Sans Fins project, to be constructed near the Grande Arche at La Défense, Paris, visualized by Georges Fessy

153

are integrated into this programme, their movements across the building silhouetted onto the facade.' Such an idea extends architecture into media, but does not confuse them.

Whatever the quality of the tools in the virtual office, and however they help the architect to communicate the idea of architecture, the architect is going to remain firmly linked both to the present and the future. The same day-to-day pressures and choices will bear down on the architect's office, the same contradictions between corporate ambition and public service, between new solutions and nostalgia for a nonexistent past. The architect's duty will remain to design not only for the present but for the future. The role of architecture goes beyond construction: it is to create visions of future ways of living, of working, of socializing. The social duty of architecture is a topic rendered dull by the pontifications of the Modern Movement, and frivolous by the antics of Post-Modernists, but it is a serious one, nonetheless. Just as a building is only one version of an architectural idea, so all architecture can be said to be virtual, and true architecture beyond the real.

There are plenty of buildings which are part of the architectural canon though they have existed hardly at all, never existed, or do not yet exist, from Mies van der Rohe's Barcelona Pavilion to Speer's Hall of the German People to Jean Nouvel's Tour Sans Fins. Design has always been for architects not merely the process of creating an actual project, but also for exploring ideas and concepts for which no client or even no building technology exists. Such images offer a challenge, inviting the viewer to consider new possibilities, new strategies. The technology that will be at the disposal of the virtual architect will help to express these new concepts and communicate them better and more completely. The convergence of virtual reality, active databases and open systems in the vision of intelligent architecture creates an opportunity for architecture to regain its role as an arbiter of the future, and it is for architects to seize that opportunity.

154

Reading List

List of Computer Companies

Index

Reading List

There are innumerable books on computing, and uncounted ones on architecture. Most major hardware ranges (such as Apple Mac and IBM PC) and computer programs (such as AutoCAD and 3D Studio, for example) also have a range of supporting books, some published by the originators of the equipment and programs, others by specialist publishing houses such as NRP and QUE. Major academic publishers also have important computer lists, which often cover CAD software, if not always from a solely architectural perspective. The list of all these specialized titles is fast-changing, as new titles are introduced to deal with new versions of programs. A visit to your computer bookstore is the best way of finding the appropriate, and current, specialist title for the application you are intending to use. Many of these specialist titles contain useful hints, detailed technical information, and many now come with free disks or CDs that carry information upgrades, specialized routines and sub-progams: they are often a worthwhile investment for the serious user.

Books dealing generally with computing and architecture, however, are few. The list that follows does not pretend to be complete: rather it is a list of the sources mentioned by the authors, as well as a number of pertinent books on the wider issues raised in this book.

Barthes, Roland, *Mythologies* (Paladin, 1979)

Benedikt, Michael (ed.), *Cyberspace: First Steps* (MIT Press, 1992)

Boal, Iain (ed.) *Resisting the Virtual Life* (City Lights Press, 1995)

Brand, Stewart, *The Media Lab: inventing the future at MIT* (Viking Penguin, 1989)

Cotton, Bob & Oliver, Richard, *The Cyberspace Lexicon* (Phaidon, 1994)

Gibson, William, *Burning Chrome*, *Count Zero*, *Mona Lisa Overdrive*, *Neuromancer* (Grafton, 1986-88)

Kreuger, Myron, *Artificial Reality* (Addison-Wesley, 1983)

Laurel, Brenda (ed.) *The Art of Human Computer Interface Design* (Addison Wesley, 1990)

Mitchell, William J., *The Reconfigured Eye* (MIT Press, 1992)

Negroponte, Nicholas, *The Architecture Machine* (MIT Press, 1970) *Being Digital* (Alfred A. Knopf, Inc, Hodder & Stoughton, 1995)

Nelson, Ted, *Computer Lib* (Tempus, 1987)

Porter, Tom, *The Architect's Eye* (Spon, 1996)

Rheingold, Harvey, *Virtual Reality* (Secker, 1991)

Thackara, John (ed.) *Design After Modernism* (Thames & Hudson, 1988)

Turner, Janet, *Lighting* (Batsford, 1994)

Weiner, Norbert *Cybernetics* (MIT Press, 1948)

Woolley, Benjamin, *Virtual Worlds: A Journey in Hype and Hyperreality* (Blackwell, Penguin, 1993).

List of Computer Companies

The computer software discussed in this book is produced by the following companies: the main headquarters country is shown in each case, but most of these products are distributed worldwide. There are also many additional options for major programs (GIS, FM, HVAC etc.), and you should consult your software supplier about the availability of particular programs in your market.

3D Studio	*Autodesk (USA)*
ArchiCAD	*Graphisoft (Hungary)*
ATMA Radiosity	*ATMA (Italy)*
AutoCAD	*Autodesk (USA)*
AutoCAD AEC	*Autodesk (USA)*
CadBau 400	*Han Dataport (Germany)*
CADSYS	*Engineering Technology (UK)*
dVISE	*Division (UK)*
dVS	*Division (UK)*
Electric Image	*Electric Image (USA)*
Infobyte	*Infobyte (Italy)*
Microstation	*Bentley Systems/Intergraph (Netherlands/USA)*
Modelshop	*Apple (USA)*
Painter	*Fractal Design (USA)*
Powerdraft	*Bentley Systems/Intergraph (Netherlands/USA)*
Reflex	*Reflex Systems (UK)*
SIMCity	*Sim Business (USA)*
SLI-WIN	*Light Consult (Germany)*
Sonata	*Alias (Canada)*
speedikon	*IEZ (Germany)*
StarARCHI	*Star (Belgium)*
Superscape	*Superscape (UK)*

Index